MONSTERS
OF WISCONSIN

Mysterious Creatures in the Badger State

Linda S. Godfrey

D1600111

STACKPOLE
BOOKS

0 11557 00748 0

Published by
STACKPOLE BOOKS
5067 Ritter Road
Mechanicsburg, PA 17055
www.stackpolebooks.com

Printed in the United States of America

10 9 8 7 6 5 4 3 2

FIRST EDITION

Cover art by Marc Radle
Cover design by Tessa J. Sweigert

Library of Congress Cataloging-in-Publication Data

Godfrey, Linda S.
  Monsters of Wisconsin : mysterious creatures in the badger state /
Linda
S. Godfrey. — 1st ed.
      p. cm.
  Includes bibliographical references.
  ISBN-13: 978-0-8117-0748-0 (pbk.)
  ISBN-10: 0-8117-0748-2 (pbk.)
  1. Monsters—New Jersey. 2. Animals, Mythical—New Jersey. I. Title.
GR825.G565 2011
398.24'54—dc22

                                    2011001932

CONTENTS

INTRODUCTION

A Monster's Ball

Wisconsin boasts forests full of impressive creatures with sharp claws and glistening fangs; cougar, bear, and eastern timber wolf populations are all on the upswing and are steadily expanding their territories. And why shouldn't they? It's easy to see why they like it here. This state is drenched in lakes and rivers and crammed full of edible plants and game. The terrain varies to suit different species, too, with dense forests in the north, cliffs and ravines that the glacier never flattened in the west, and great prairies-turned-cornfields in the south and east. Those very same attributes, though, may also attract lesser-known creatures that a zoologist could not classify.

The list of Wisconsin unknowns is daunting: Bigfoot, werewolves, man bats, goat men, Thunderbirds, dragons, lizard men, the Hodag, aliens, hell hounds, and even urban kangaroos. With the exception of one kangaroo and a wallaby, most of these impossible beasts are never captured, seldom photographed except as blob-shadows, and never quite pinned down tightly enough that we may examine the stuff of which they are made. They are all very talented at squirming away or vanishing.

Despite the best efforts of observers and investigators, then, we still haven't the foggiest notion of what these creatures actually are. We only know that people ranging in time from the first indigenous nations to contemporary travelers on six-lane freeways have claimed to have seen them. Many have afterwards wished they had not.

Over the years, a historical blend of native peoples have called this state home: Ojibwe, Potawatomi, Ho-Chunk, Sac, Fox, and the mysterious vanished traders we call Mississippians are a few well-known tribal affiliations. Although some of these people have been in Wisconsin longer than others, all of them share traditions of hairy manlike creatures, giant birds, and fearsome water monsters.

When Europeans began to populate the state, they brought their own well-rounded panoply of spooky beings. Werewolves were one of the earliest, sailing into the Great Lakes with early French traders and trappers and then hitching rides in later centuries with emigrant Germans. The British and Irish brought hellhounds and fairy dogs, the Slavs their vampires, and Belgians their strange pig men that wrought curses for vengeful Door County farmers. Sea monsters followed the ships of all of them to explore the shores of New England and adapt to fresh inland waters, where they joined the lake creatures that had always been here.

The magical thing that all of these peoples have had in common is a history of telling stories. The stories are what keep strange beasts alive. You see, although more than a few of these creatures have built their reputations on their desire to eat human flesh, physical meat is not what they crave most. Their true food is the human word. Our words about them are their feast. And that feast grants them a sort of immortality that will keep them lurking around in the bushes until our very last storyteller dies.

In many ways, our monsters are us. And that may be why we love them so.

Mr. Big, or Sasquatch in Dairyland

The huge, apelike creature called Bigfoot or Sasquatch might be considered the world's most popular monster. It has starred in countless TV commercials and movies and has inspired hundreds of organizations and websites devoted to finding Bigfoot and proving its existence. Believers argue endlessly over whether it would be okay to kill one, what the creatures eat, and whether it's better to stalk them alone by sitting quietly in the woods or go en masse with a group all banging sticks on trees and bellowing their best imitations of great ape calls.

Not everyone believes. Despite evidence, including plaster casts of footprints with such hard-to-fake features as unique skin or dermal ridges, hair samples that can't be pinned on any known species, and hundreds of eyewitness reports, many pooh-pooh the existence of what some call the Sasquatch. Those who do advance the possibility that a giant species of unknown primate—perhaps one that is closer to humans in intelligence than any other great ape—roams the Americas and other parts of the world may expect mockery and catcalls for their efforts.

Controversy continues to rage over the authenticity of what is called the Patterson-Gimlin film. Shot in California in 1967, the one-minute clip shows what looks like a female, hair-covered hominoid striding along, arms swinging in a rather non-human way. But a scientific analysis of the creature's movement and anatomy by Idaho State University associate professor of anatomy and anthropology, Dr. Jeff Meldrum, in his book, *Sasquatch: Legend Meets Science*, puts forth tantalizing evidence that Bigfoot may be real.

Meldrum, who has endured his own share of disbelief from fellow scientists, says that recent foot and body imprint casts have been "pivotal in turning the heads of noted primate anatomists and dermatoglyphists." He adds in his book, "Expert viewers could not casually dismiss a number of films and videos as simply an obvious case of a 'man in a fur suit.'" And Meldrum's studies have inspired him to speculate that "the legend of sasquatch possibly has its basis in a real animal and may eventually prove to be among the most astounding zoological discoveries ever." Perhaps that discovery will be made in Wisconsin!

Of course, there are others who think Bigfoot is "real" in an unreal way: a furry traveler from another place or time, or even a Chewbacca-like alien on furlough from its UFO.

A growing number of Wisconsinites, however, don't need professional opinions or paranormal theories to convince them that an eight-foot-tall, hairy hominoid stomps the woods and marshes of Wisconsin. They've seen it. Their ranks include middle-aged married couples, restaurant owners, newspaper deliverers, hunters, and fishermen, to name a few of the diverse types of people brave enough to report what they saw.

Sharp-eyed folk have spotted the giant creatures running through the Chequamegon National Forest in the state's far north and hiding in barns and tree lines of a specific range of swampy, forested land in Jefferson, Rock, and Walworth Counties in the south. None of the people I've talked to have felt that Bigfoot wanted to attack them; in almost every case the creature just keeps on truckin'. And in this day of eager monster hunters, that is probably just what the big fella needs to do to survive.

The Lima Marsh Monster

Lenny and Stacie Faytus were not out looking for Bigfoot the day their worldview changed forever. The forty-three-year-old husband and thirty-nine-year-old wife were on their way to a pet-sitting job on McCord Road at the edge of the northeast corner of Rock County in the late spring of 2005. The time was about an hour before sunset, and the couple was enjoying the rustic scenery along the drive.

They noticed a farmer in a field next to the road and remarked to one another how strange it was that he had turned on every light on his tractor, with a few spotlights added, even though the sun still shone brightly. Then they saw what may have caused the farmer to ramp up his wattage. Ahead in the distance, something tall and dark stepped out of a dense cluster of trees and onto the road. Lenny kept driving, wondering whether it was an animal or a person. But as he drew closer, he decided it was neither.

He described it as upright and of medium-brown color, walking quickly but easily on two legs. Lenny realized as the creature ducked behind a road sign that it stood at least seven feet tall and weighed a minimum of 350 pounds, probably more. It had crossed the twenty-foot-wide road in only two long strides. Lenny could make out a humanoid face, with no muzzle, and fur that obscured its ears and neck.

Stacie had seen it, too, and both of them felt the hair rise up on their arms and the backs of their necks. By then they were almost to the spot where the creature had crossed. As they reached it, Lenny craned for another glimpse of the creature, but it was nowhere to be seen. He realized at that moment that the creature had quickly hidden itself and was probably watching them, aware it had been seen. The road on that side dropped into a four-foot-deep depression, filled with weeds and backed by a cultivated field. The Bigfoot—and Lenny and Stacie are sure that's what it was—had most likely flattened itself in that ditch.

The Faytuses never reported their sighting to the authorities and kept it mostly to themselves. Not long after seeing the creature, they bought a restaurant in that same area called the Richmond House. The place happens to be one of the author's favorite spots for fried fish, and Lenny decided to mention the incident one Friday night. Otherwise, I probably would never have heard of it. They have kept a very low profile and have done nothing to call attention to their experience. The fact that the sighting was in daylight and they both had a good look at the creature rules out explanations like hallucination, misidentification, and the like.

Two other things: The accompanying terrain and a slew of corroborating reports put this sighting into the category of "very interesting." McCord Road lies just east of a large, wild swamp area called the Lima Marsh. The two-mile road is also sandwiched between Lake Koshkonong and North and Whitewater Lakes, which back up into the southern unit of the dense Kettle Moraine State Forest. It's a very rural area with many small, lightly traveled roads and a good supply of deer, pheasants, turkey, and other small game, not to mention the occasional henhouse and cornfield to pilfer. A large, hardy omnivore could conceivably raise a small family here.

Then there are the other sightings. Only about a month before the Faytus sighting, on March 9, 2005, a UW–Whitewater student returning home to Lima Center from her late-night job at a movie theater was heading west on State Highway 59 near the Lima Marsh Wildlife Area when she saw a tall, dark, and hairy creature standing by the side of the highway. That was just a few miles from McCord Road.

In 1999, halfway between Elkhorn and Whitewater near North Lake and only a scant twelve miles from Lima Center, a Chicago computer salesman named Joe was on his way to fish at the lake. He was about a mile north of Millard on County Highway O when he noticed movement on the east side of the road through his passenger window.

He slowed down and saw a seven-foot, 400-pound creature walking through the tall grass in the ditch, swinging its long arms from big shoulders and leaning slightly forward as if intent on where it was going. It was covered in "rust brown" fur that appeared uneven and unkempt, and as it turned its head to look at him, Joe said his first thought was, "Whoa, that is not a person!"

His second thought was, "Don't stop the car."

The creature's eyes were "sunken into" the fur that covered its face, he said, and no ears or muzzle were visible. He said it reminded him of Chewbacca from *Star Wars*. He kept on driving and did not look back, and he never told anyone about it. He is not a seeker of the supernatural, he said, but found the author's website while browsing the Internet and decided to write.

Other Southern Wisconsin Sightings

There is a surprising backlist of additional sightings in this general area of the state between 1964 and 2010.

In 1964, a middle-aged Delavan man driving home from work saw a dark, fur-covered creature he identified as a Bigfoot standing in a cornfield to his left, just north of Richmond Townline Road. The creature leaped over a four-foot-plus fence and then ran upright across the road in front of the man's astonished eyes, swinging its long arms. He estimated the creature stood seven to eight feet tall and weighed between 400 and 500 pounds. No ears or snout were visible, and while the creature appeared humanoid in shape, the man was sure it was not a big, hairy human.

The man seemed extremely credible. I interviewed him in person several times and also wrote a completely unrelated newspaper article about his main passion, an astonishing soda bottle collection that filled his entire basement. The man has been grilled by other researchers but his account of what he saw that night has never changed over the forty-plus years that have since passed.

In the 1970s, a region centered around Bluff Road in southern Jefferson County, in the heart of the Kettle Moraine State Forest Southern Unit, became known as the home of the Bluff Monster. Two women who grew up around Palmyra, Judy Wallerman and Rochelle Kemp, described seeing a Bigfoot-like creature on several occasions just off County Highway H on a large rise called Young Hill.

The sightings occurred when the women were teenagers. The hill was lit with a huge star every December, and they could sometimes see the creature illuminated by the electric lights of the decoration. Wallerman drew a rough sketch for me of a hairy, long-armed humanlike creature, a classic Bigfoot. She said they would sit out at night and watch for it, and they would see it darting over the hill as if it were chasing something. Other students from their high school also saw the creature, said Wallerman.

The women's claims are supported by the fact that I had heard rumors of the Bluff Monster from other people for years. In nearby East Troy it was called the Eddy, probably a corruption of the word for a similar beast seen in the Himalayas, the "Yeti." A woman who grew up in East Troy told me that cruising around the area between East Troy and Palmyra to look for the Eddy was a standard dating ritual.

About that same time in the 1970s, a woman who lived in Jefferson County in rural Fort Atkinson called a Department of Natural Resources (DNR) officer to report that she had seen a tall, hairy, apelike creature skulking around the buildings on her farm. Agent David Gjetson drove out to investigate but reported that he didn't find anything suspicious.

Two weeks later, however, Gjetson received another call from the woman. The creature was back, she said, and its behavior had escalated. First, the beast marched up to her front door and shook it, as if demanding entry. As the woman cowered in her kitchen, the creature then slashed the frame seven feet above the porch level with its claws. Then it ran to the barn and attacked a horse tethered inside, slashing its neck open, before stomping off through the woman's garden. She said the animal left big tracks, although Gjetson said he had found no evidence of the footprints when I interviewed him by phone. He did say he felt the woman was sincere, and he added the welcome news that the horse survived.

Many Bigfoot researchers feel that the creatures are attracted to horses, although often in a more benign way. Michigan writer Lisa Shiel, for instance, claims in her book *Backyard Bigfoot* that a Bigfoot frequently visited her horse barn to tie intricate braids in her horses' tails and manes. But equine braiding is a phenomenon that has gone on for centuries in many places; in England it was blamed on fairies. Even Shakespeare wrote that fairy ruler Queen Mab "plaits the manes of horses in the night." The French blamed it on another form of mischievous little people called "the lutin."

Human horse groomers sometimes call these puzzling phenomena "witch's knots." But they generally agree, I learned after visiting a great number of horse care Internet sites, that most of these tangles are made either by horses rubbing their lips across one another's manes and tails, or by the long hairs winding around small burrs or even rolling together as the horse repetitively rubs against a wall or tree or flicks its tail at bothersome flies.

It should be noted that no hairs were found braided on the Jefferson County farm horse—just a long and ugly wound.

River Watcher

One summer Saturday in 1980, Walworth resident Ronald Nixon drove to the northwest corner of Walworth County to angle for catfish on the Bark River. The river flows through a marshy state wildlife area perhaps eight miles northeast of Lima Center and was a favorite fishing spot of Nixon's.

As Nixon sat in his boat, baiting his hook with "stinky cheese," he happened to glimpse a big, dark, hairy creature crouching, as a human would crouch, near some weeds. When it realized Nixon had seen it, the creature moved back into the shadows. Nixon went home and told his wife he had seen a "yeti." That was the last time he fished there alone. She shared the story with me years later, after he died.

Barely a mile or two north of the Bark River is the tiny community of Hebron. In 1993, eight-year old Andrew Hurd and a friend of his went out to play in an unused barn on the family's rural farm on Fromader Road. It was summer and early afternoon on a sunny day. But as Andrew entered the barn, he heard a noise to his right and saw a dark figure that looked larger than a human. The creature was no mere shadow; it sprinted bipedally through the barn, running hunched over as if to keep a low profile. Hurd said it was very fast.

Hurd ran the other way, screaming that something was in the barn. His parents called police, who told the family there had been other reports nearby (none of which made the local newspapers).

Andrew was twenty-two when he told me about his experience, and he said he still remembered the creature's face. Its head and face were covered with dark hair, and the nose appeared ape-like. What scared him even more was that the police found a circular area in the tall grass behind the barn that looked like something very large had bedded down there.

Cavemen or Teenage Bigfoot?

One odd Whitewater area sighting that *may* have been a Bigfoot occurred in September 2008, near 10 P.M., as several young people drove past Whitewater's artesian well, a stone structure that has flowed since 1895 on Clover Valley Road.

"It darted out at us," wrote the driver. "I was worried it was going to jump on our trunk, but it did not. We were very scared because we were not sure what it was. It kind of looked like a caveman."

Three years earlier, in September 2005, Matt Wakely saw something he also described as like a caveman on the opposite side of Walworth County, on White Pigeon Road near the Wisconsin-Illinois state line. The twenty-one-year-old was driving home from work at about two o'clock on a sunny afternoon when he noticed a figure standing in the old settlers' cemetery at White Pigeon and County Highway B, between Geneva Lake and Pell Lake. The figure was tall and shaped like a human, but had shaggy hair all over its body, with an especially wild shock—tall and shaggy—on top of its head. It stood nonchalantly with one foot up on a tombstone and watched Wakely as the startled young man drove slowly past.

At first Wakely thought the being watching him from the cemetery tree line was some strange, naked human, but realized he was wrong when he drew closer. Its fur was chocolate-colored, Wakely said, and it stood with one hand on its hip and the other arm hanging at its side to about the middle of its thigh. It was taller than an average adult human male, said Wakely, but was not big-chested or brawny in the way Bigfoot are usually described.

Wakely added that the creature's roundish face with a flat, wide nose reminded him of the cavemen in the Geico Insurance television ads. It turned its head to continue observing

Wakely as he passed it. Wakely said he considered turning the car around to have another look, but the creature appeared wild enough that he was afraid it might charge the car. With that cautionary thought in mind, he kept going and called his mom on his cell phone instead.

Wakely's mother was the one who contacted me to report the incident, and she said her son called her to say he thought he had seen a caveman.

One possibility is that these "cavemen" are actually juvenile Bigfoot, which would naturally be smaller and perhaps feature immature hair growth. If Bigfoot is a real, physical creature, young ones would necessarily exist.

The description also sounds like something Bigfoot researchers Loren Coleman and Patrick Huyghe call an Erectus Hominid in their book *The Field Guide to Bigfoot, Yeti, and Other Mystery Primates Worldwide.*

Could it have been a human in a fur suit? Wakely didn't think so; the fur was too unevenly distributed and the face was not like that of a modern human. Wakely also passed a professionally administered polygraph that proved he was indeed convinced of what he saw in the cemetery that bright day. The polygraph expert's official conclusion: no deception indicated.

The Honey Creek Hurdler

It was 1994 when Honey Creek residents David and Mary Pagliaroni received the scare of their lives as they drove home one night after a nice restaurant dinner. They were approaching the Honey Creek Bridge from County Highway DD on the eastern side of Walworth County, about twenty-five miles southeast of Hebron. Near the spot where Honey Lake and Honey Creek meet up, something tall and reddish stepped out onto the bridge, illuminated by their headlights.

David, then forty-five, and Mary, forty-four, stared at the hulking, fur-covered creature that stood only about twenty feet in front of them. David hit the brakes.

"It froze right in the headlights and just stood there, leaning over and looking at us," David told me in an interview at their home. He and the creature made eye contact.

"The eyes were black; they didn't reflect the headlights . . . the hair came down off the head and formed almost a little mini-cape; you could see where the hair all ended," he said.

The creature's long arms hung well below its "waist," said David, and it appeared larger and heavier than a human. No ears were visible, and its face was flat and ape-like. The creature continued to stare into David's eyes for a few seconds, and then turned to take a few steps toward a bridge railing. What it did next astonished the Pagliaronis even more.

The creature put one hair-covered hand—David insisted it was a hand with fingers and thumb, not a paw—on the concrete bridge railing, swung both legs over the rail, and then dropped easily to the creekbed fifteen to twenty feet below, where the Pagliaronis could no longer see it. David noted that its feet were also heavily fur-covered and that it had no tail. He drew a sketch that showed an upright, apelike creature leaning toward their car.

Mary noted that although she and David never had any problem sharing their feelings about things, neither said a word about what they had seen for weeks. David said he just wanted to leave the area.

"There was something about it I didn't want to go after," he said. He noted that despite the fact that he was a Vietnam War veteran and an avid hunter and outdoorsman, his instincts told him to leave this creature to itself.

David and Mary both passed polygraph tests administered by an expert for History Channel's *Monsterquest* as part of their "American Werewolf" episode. (The same expert tested Wakely, above.) Their encounter was reenacted on the show, although the production did not make it clear that what the couple saw was apelike rather than canine. David and Mary, however, have no doubt to this day that they saw Bigfoot.

The Holy Hill Dog-Napper

The area of Washington County around a Catholic shrine called Holy Hill became nationally famous in the fall of 2006, after a contractor for the state DNR saw an unidentified, upright canine steal a deer carcass out of the back of his pickup truck. That story is covered in this book's werewolf section. But other tall and hairy things have also been seen in this hilly, forested, and well-watered terrain. And deer are not their only prey.

Between 11 A.M. and noon on a warm spring day in the late 1980s, Ross Tamms and his girlfriend decided to take a cruise around the scenic area. He does not remember the exact road they were on, but they were admiring a farmhouse set into an evergreen-covered hillside when they noticed what looked like a "brown clump" at the edge of the driveway to that house. Neither could identify it at first glance, and Tamms slowed his car to a crawl as they approached.

"As we drove by," he wrote in an e-mail, "I was so alarmed by what I was seeing I just about drove us off the road." He turned to ask his girlfriend if she knew what it was, but she was sitting with her hands on the dash, her face frozen and white. He asked again whether she also saw the large brown "thing" kneeling and holding out its massive arms, and she managed to say yes. Tamms replied, "But we are the only species that kneels."

He was shaken, he said, from the fact that he stared straight into the creature's "black, very human-like eyes." He added that he could clearly see the whites around the black pupils as the creature tracked the path of their passing car. "It almost looked surprised," he said, "like it just got its hands caught in the cookie jar."

And well it might have. The large hands held out in front of it contained not a cookie but a small, black-and-white dog that appeared dead to Tamms and his girlfriend. The girlfriend had the impression that the creature was sad that the dog was dead, but Tamms said he was sure the dog was intended to be the creature's next meal, perhaps stolen from the farm. The creature was definitely large enough to kill a dog, according to Tamms's description.

"This thing was huge," he said. "I was working in plumbing back then and I had a very good eye for measurements. It definitely had humanistic qualities. It had very broad shoulders and not much of a neck (at least it seemed because of its hair). The hair was three to four inches long all over its body, seemingly uniform. It was definitely reddish brown. The face was black, almost masklike, something like that of a great ape.

"As we passed and because our windows had been slightly open, an incredible odor entered the car. It was so foul, I asked (my girlfriend) if she had passed gas. But in reality the stench was so bad that both of us literally felt as if we were going to get sick."

Tamms's girlfriend wanted to go back to confirm what they had seen. He says he replied, "Over my dead body. We are going this way and the faster we go the safer I feel!"

Tamms added, "We passed by this thing around noon on a very bright day and it was on the side of the road—no trees or shrubs obstructing our view. So at the very most it was twenty to twenty-five feet from us."

Bigfoot of the Chequamegon

Wisconsinite and outdoorsman Dan Watring, author of *Republican Quail and Other Great Outdoor Stories*, shared one hunting tale that few other sportsmen could equal (also excerpted in my *Strange Wisconsin: More Badger State Weirdness*.) Watring said that he and his friend Dick were prowling for grouse in the Chequamegon-Nicolet National Forest, a vast preserve covering more than 1.5 million acres, when a very unexpected target came into view.

The great forest meanders through five Wisconsin counties, from Bayfield to Vilas, and harbors a diverse patchwork of landscapes from boggy marsh to ghost logging camps. Watring would not reveal exactly where he was hunting, other than that it was in an ideal habitat for grouse and near one of those abandoned logging camps. He and Dick found their way into the area through the right-of-way to a major electric power line. They spent the day hunting with their dogs until rain forced them to take a break.

As they waited out the showers by driving slowly through a tamarack bog, they suddenly spotted a tall, manlike creature covered in dark fur staring at them from about forty yards away. Watring estimated the beast stood seven feet tall, with a massive chest, a sturdy build, and long arms that ended in big, hairy hands.

After a few moments, the creature strode quickly across the road and disappeared into a nearby thicket. Watring described its gait as "rolling," but similar to a human's. As the dogs growled, the two men got out of the vehicle, and Watring, shaken, grabbed his rifle and loaded it, watching all the while in case the creature came back. It did not return, and the men decided to drop any brave notions of chasing after it.

The pair confided in a friend whose uncle was a Native American tribal elder in that area, said Watring, and the uncle told them that the "spirit man thing" had been known to his people for many years, that there was more than one of them, and that his own father and grandfather had seen them. He also said they believed it best to leave the "dark spirit man" alone, said Watring.

This was very consistent with what other indigenous people have told me their traditions say about the hairy unknowns. They believe that Bigfoot can travel between worlds by the use of special entrances or portals and that is why dead specimens are never found.

One particular aspect of Watring's amazing experience caught my attention: the proximity of major power lines. Such lines also run through a preserve in southern Rock County where witnesses saw several upright doglike creatures. Some researchers have theorized that powerful electromagnetic fields may interact with human minds to either produce hallucinations or to make visible entities that are normally beyond our ability to see. Whether the power lines played a role or not, the creature certainly looked very real to Watring.

Clark County Colossus

One common thread of many Bigfoot encounters is that the creatures are often glimpsed going about what looks like the procurement of animal protein, either chasing down prey or carrying a hunk of carrion off to a more secluded dining area. That was the case in Clark County near Granton around 5 A.M. on the morning of March 28, 2000, as a rural newspaper carrier happened upon a Bigfoot toting its breakfast: a goat-sized chunk of some dead thing.

The fifty-seven-year-old former long-haul trucker was distributing the *Clark County Press and Shopper* when he saw what he described as a "big hairy ape of some kind," first crossing the road and then stopping to stare at him.

"It turned and looked at me," he said in a phone interview in June 2006, "and my blood turned to ice. I saw two dark spots where the eyes would be. It had something in its right hand that could have been roadkill or part of a deer carcass; it was about the size of a goat. It was well over eight feet high and if it didn't weight five hundred pounds it didn't weigh an ounce. The shape of the top of the head would be compared to a gorilla. It had long, grayish-colored hair that was honey-colored in some spots. No ears, nothing like that, he was just all long hair. I couldn't tell where the neck was."

The witness did not notice any odor, but had the windows rolled up to ward off the morning chill. The creature was about a half mile away from him when he first spotted it walking across County Highway H. He kept driving until he reached the creature, which was on the south side of the road with its back to him.

Thinking he was doing the right thing, he later reported his sighting to the county sheriff, meaning that the local newspaper found out. The man's comment that the carcass the creature carried was about the size of a goat was misquoted. The papers all said that the Bigfoot carried a dead goat, and the story hit news outlets worldwide.

Having talked to the man both on the phone and in person, I can say that he is a reluctant witness and has not sought any sort of fame or reward for the incident. "Until I seen this thing I was skeptical," he said. "I wouldn't have said anything except my wife and her girlfriend talked me into it. I said I didn't know what the hell it was."

The sheriff's deputy who examined the scene did not find any tracks because the ground was too hard, the man said. The man went back to the area himself a few days later and stood on the spot where the creature had stopped and turned, but did not see anything he could use as proof, either.

The man said he refused to go on local TV. "I really didn't want the notoriety," he said. "I hope I never see another one, especially not that close." And although his name appeared in multiple outlets, he asked me not to use it and I am honoring that request.

"If I ever see another one," he told me on June 16, 2006, over burgers in a Marshfield café, "I'm going to shut my mouth."

Lugerville

At least two men have reported encounters with Bigfoot while hunting just two counties north of Marshfield outside of the near-ghost town of Lugerville in Price County. One was reported in 1997 on the website of the Bigfoot Research Organization (BFRO). A man hunting in the rugged terrain from a tree stand saw a dark figure walking on a ridge about one hundred yards away, accompanied by the sound of large branches snapping.

Another man who lives in that area, a hunting and fishing guide named Don Young, said he saw a creature several times over the past decade or two. The reports from the two men were enough to bring both the BFRO and the History Channel show *Monsterquest* for expeditions. The TV crew was able to find a large bedding area where something impervious to sharp sawgrass had chewed and beaten down the vegetation, and the BFRO team acquired unverified thermal images, but Bigfoot did not show his humanoid face to either group.

Anyone who knows that country can understand how even a very large creature could hide itself well in the swamps and woods, and many Bigfoot researchers have speculated that the creatures can smell cameras from miles away.

The Deltox Marsh Monster

It only seems appropriate that one of Wisconsin's best-known Bigfoot sightings, chronicled in the April 1969 issue of *Argosy* magazine, should have occurred where the Wolf and Rat Rivers meet. That would be in northern Winnebago County, just north of Lake Poygan, in a former sedge meadow-turned-swamp called the Deltox Marsh.

A total of fifteen different witnesses claimed to have seen the creature that the article's writer, Ivan Sanderson, called the ABSM or Abominable Snowman. Sanderson and zoologist Dr. Bernard Heuvelmans of Belgium's Royal Institute of Natural Sciences traveled to the wild area west of Neenah–Menasha to interview twelve deer hunters in January 1969. The hunters had all caught varying glimpses of a tall, humanlike creature covered in short, dark fur, walking upright and swinging very long arms, while on a deer drive on November 30, 1968. Three of those twelve had also spotted the creature on another hunting expedition a little more than a month earlier, on October 19. And at least three more witnesses came forward later.

The twelve hunters ranged in age from only twelve years old to sixty-seven, said Sanderson. He and Heuvelmans questioned all of them closely on a tape recorder, and the men described how they began their march through the swamp, about twenty feet apart from each other, in an attempt to flush any deer out into the open. That meant they were at differing distances from the creature when the three men closest to it spied the behemoth standing in grass that measured three to four feet tall.

The creature's torso stood well above the top of the grass stalks. They noticed that its face was a lighter color than the fur and had little to no hair on it, and that they could not see a neck. Although some of the hunters had shorter glimpses and were farther away, the entire group agreed that the creature was sturdily built with big shoulders and a "barrel-shaped" chest. They all insisted that it did not look nor move like a bear, and instead reminded them of an apelike human.

The men halted their drive and tried to track the creature, but it was able to walk into some dense undergrowth and did not reappear. None of them even considered shooting it because its appearance was so manlike.

The three who had seen the creature earlier during archery season were Bob Parry, Dick Bleier, and Bill Mallo. Parry had the best view of it from his tree stand while the others gawked from the ground. On that occasion they also first spotted it standing and then watched it move quickly on two legs to "dance" behind a stand of brush.

The two investigators asked whether the creature might have been a human in a "monkey suit" running around the swamp, but since the event occurred in hunting season the twelve men practically laughed Sanderson and Heuvelmans out of the campfire circle. Anyone who tried that with so many trigger-happy hunters in the woods would have to be suicidal, they said.

That same fall, the creature was also seen in the area by a Mr. Freeman, and was spotted on a roadside by a Mr. and Mrs. Stan Penkala, according to Sanderson's article. Sanderson also noted that while he and Heuvelmans were still on site, four "young local men" volunteered to show them some tracks that they said had been found in the snow by unnamed children.

Sanderson thought the seventeen-inch-long tracks looked man-made and they probably were; it sounds like the young people knew investigators were in town and took advantage of the situation to have some fun with it. But while the track hoax did cast a pall over the sightings, it did not disprove them. And the report remains one of the largest group sightings ever.

Spring Green Rock Chucker

How does an eight-foot-tall, five-hundred-pound creature hide in plain sight? One incident near Spring Green suggests Bigfoot might just play possum—standing up.

Spring Green, set along the Wisconsin River in Sauk County, boasts one of the state's most scenic locales as well as a top tourist attraction: the uniquely designed, mammoth faux museum known as The House on the Rock. The area may also boast a Bigfoot population.

A family that asked to remain unnamed rented a farmhouse north of the town around 2001 and was puzzled when they began to find odd shreds of deer fur near their house and a pile of five or six deer carcasses stashed behind a tree. Their home was in a valley between the little burgs of Plain and Bear Valley, in a hilly, creek-fed area.

Then the husband and the couple's daughter glimpsed something large and covered in reddish fur hustle into the woods, growling loudly at them as it went. They began to think something truly unusual was living near them. That was about to be confirmed.

The wife was weeding a fence line one day when she said it was as if she heard a message inside of her telling her to get in the house. She resisted and kept on weeding. The next thing she knew, rocks coming from the direction of the woods began plunking onto the tin roof of a nearby springhouse. Again she heard an interior voice commanding her to leave. Finally a neighbor's dog began to bark in a frenzied way and she took the hint to skedaddle.

The corker came in summer of that year when some friends from Chicago drove up to visit them. The friends were curious about something they had seen. Why, they asked, did the neighbors have a statue of some tall, hairy creature standing in their front yard? Everyone piled in the car to go have a look, but the neighbor's yard was empty. The "statue" had disappeared.

Town of Frankfort Freakiness

The introduction to this chapter mentioned that some people think Bigfoot and UFOs are somehow related. Some think both are manifestations of the same, all-pervading other-dimensional or spirit entity. Others think UFOS are bringing the Bigfoot.

According to two articles from the *Wausau Daily Herald* posted on the *W-Files* website, a *Marshfield News-Herald* story, and an article in the *Abbottsford Tribune-Phonograph*, a town of Frankfort resident named Rita Massman did think UFOs had something to do with the eight-foot-tall Bigfoot her children saw on several occasions near their home in July 1991. A neighbor had seen a UFO, she explained to a *Herald* reporter, and then the Bigfoot began to make his presence known.

Because Bigfoot's true nature is really unknown, and because the creature seems to prefer to hide rather than attack, some people have come to think of the creature almost affectionately. Investigators call this the *Harry and the Hendersons* syndrome, referring to the film about a family that adopts a Sasquatch. The Massmans' experience involved a creature that seemed to have adopted *them*, in a shadowy sort of way.

Neither Massman nor her husband Klaus actually laid eyes on the creature, but their four children cited five separate sightings between July 11 and 17 of that year. One boy, Raimund, said he saw it three times, starting on the 11th. He first heard a strange "clapping" sound in the woods, then noticed his dog making fearful "squeaking" sounds. Then he saw a tall, gray-furred creature run toward the shed where Raimund had just put away his bicycle. It was as tall as the eave on the shed, said Raimund, and the eave is eight feet above the ground. It stopped and looked at the boy, and Raimund said he could see its eyes and a nose. Then it ran back into the woods. Raimund saw it near the shed another time, and also saw it run past his bedroom window while he was resting in bed one day after accidentally burning his hand.

Rita Massman said she felt that it watched her when she worked outside on their thickly forested, eighty-acre property on the Big Eau Pleine River, perfect territory for large, strange creatures. When their penned chickens started to disappear despite a gate that required fingers to open it, they called the sheriff and requested both the United States Army and the state DNR be called in to conduct a high-tech search of the land. The sheriff did call the DNR and the Massmans gave the sheriff's department a fur shred they had found on a shrub to examine, but the official who came to the farm said only that it could be from a dog and confiscated it. An *Abbotsford Tribune-Phonograph* reporter who called the Marathon County sheriff's investigators that took the sample said they did not return his calls.

The Massmans kept finding trampled areas they believed had been made by the gray giant, and Klaus Massman said that he heard something big stalking him when he went in the woods, something that stopped and waited quietly every time he stopped. The Massmans were afraid for their children and stopped giving them a free run of the farm. They even resorted to homemade alarms, such as a rope strung across the ground with various noisemakers, and began carrying a pistol or knife when outside. They figured, however, that the creature would be too smart to entangle itself in any trap. They were right, of course.

After a year, said a *Herald* article by reporter Chuck Baldwin, a psychic who heard about the family's fright came to communicate telepathically with the unseen invader and told it to leave. It appeared to do so, the Massmans agreed. As far as I know, that was the end of their ordeal; perhaps E.T. phoned home.

Interestingly, I had another report of a creature seen in conjunction with strange lights that behaved oddly. It also occurred in the 1990s, just north of the Marathon County line and near the Little Eau Pleine River. A group of teen boys that spent a lot of time outdoors first observed very bright, close lights before a bizarre creature began to appear, acting as if it was watching them over the course of a year or so. It stood more than six feet tall on two clawed feet, with large yellow slanted eyes, upright pointed ears, and grayish-tan skin. It could run on two or four feet. I don't think it sounds like a Bigfoot, but the fact that the young men repeatedly saw strange lights when the creature was around in that very same part of the state lends some corroboration to the Massmans' claims. The full creature report is titled "The Wausau Whatzit" in my *Strange Wisconsin*.

Cashton's Dairy-Loving Bigfoot

A farmer near the little town of Cashton, about twenty-five miles east of La Crosse, reported a Bigfoot with a craving for dairy products visited him in the fall of 1976. The Bigfoot incident was recorded by Terry Burt and Cashton resident Bud Cavadini, who wrote a series of articles in the *La Crosse Tribune* that also described an earlier encounter between a Bigfoot and an anonymous Cashton dairy man.

The sighting was not recent; it dated back to around 1950. That year, the farmer said he and his dog got up for milking chores one morning and saw the eight-foot-tall creature standing amid his herd of cows. The farmer described the usual dark hair that covered the creature's body, along with big, muscular shoulders and a humanoid but apelike face. It smelled very rank, he said, and unlike the cows, it stood and walked on two legs. The farmer did not say whether the creature sported a telltale milk mustache.

Human and humanoid stood in mutual shock at one another's presence, but the protective farm dog took action. It dashed at the great creature only to be swatted away like a bug. That was enough for the dog, which ran for the house. Evidently it was enough for the creature, too. It stepped neatly over the barbed-wire fence that enclosed the cow pen and strode quickly out of sight on its two thick legs.

The farmer and a companion tried hunting the creature with rifles in the section of the woods where it had taken refuge. They heard it snapping twigs and grunting and could smell its distinctive, skunky odor. They even felt that it was circling them, but it managed to stay out of the men's sight. (This seemed very similar to Klaus Massman's experience forty-one years later.)

That one encounter of the cow kind was the only actual sighting, but other supporting incidents involved the farmer hearing heavy hay bales moving and then finding them mysteriously rearranged in the barn, and smelling that same rotten odor on the cows after they had been outdoors all night.

The farmer and his family eventually moved away, and since no more has been heard of the Cashton Bigfoot, it probably did too.

Phantom Bigfoot

A University of Wisconsin professor, writing under the pen name of Lunetta Woods, has assembled in her book *Story in the Snow* one of the strangest chronicles of Bigfoot-human interaction ever written. The book's foreword promises a different outlook on the hairy hominoids when it teases, "If you believe in angels, you will believe in Sasquatch."

Angels, as most people know, are spiritual beings that can appear in solid flesh to carry out their main purpose as God's messengers to humanity. The very same description applies to the creatures Woods claims to have contacted on her rural Wisconsin property. They are bigger and hairier than human-sized angels and lack wings (although so do almost all mentions of Biblical angels), but otherwise have much in common with heavenly visitors, says Woods.

One of the main points of the book, which is written from the perspective of a multi-dimensional Sasquatch named Yesoda, is that Bigfoot has the ability to shape shift into other animal forms, such as a deer, a hawk, or even a hummingbird. Yesoda and her male counterpart, Kunta, proved this to Woods and her family by leaving footprints in the snow that began as super-sized humanoid prints but trailed into large deer tracks. Woods also felt that the two Sasquatch sometimes appeared to her in the guise of more ordinary animals. They also sometimes revealed themselves by releasing a skunky odor or sending a whistling sound from the nearby woods.

Woods sees the Bigfoot creatures both as spiritual guardians of her family and as messengers warning of earth changes to come. In the book, Yesoda announces that she and other Bigfoot are prepared to guide "spiritually evolved" people either to safety underground or to enter interdimensional portals to assure their survival from Earth's coming cataclysms.

This point of view is quite different from the position of many Bigfoot research groups, which believe firmly that Bigfoot is a wholly physical, highly intelligent primate yet unknown to mainstream science. Their most common going theory is that these creatures are descended from some Old World primate that crossed the Bering Strait along with early humans and has survived by avoiding humans as much as possible. A pongid named *Gigantopithecus* is the species cited most often to support this idea. This ape lived one million to

300,000 years ago in what is now China and Southeast Asia and would have stood around ten feet tall if it had walked upright. It appears to have been a knuckle-walker like today's gorilla, however.

Skeptics of the flesh-and-blood Bigfoot theory find it hard to believe that such large animals could survive in numbers sufficient for a breeding population without leaving definite proof of their existence—or even one dead body or skeleton. Internationally respected researcher Nick Redfern has another idea a bit closer to that of Lunetta Woods. As he states in *Memoirs of a Monster Hunter*, Redfern believes "that Bigfoot, and the many and varied cryptozoological mysteries that continue to both fascinate and flummox us, were paranormal." Or at least, he adds, the creatures have powerful mental abilities that can make us believe they are supernatural.

This side of the crypto-coin is supported by the fact that wherever strange creatures are seen, other strange creatures and strange phenomena like UFOs, ghosts, and mystery lights are also likely to occur (such as in the previous story about the Massman farm in the town of Frankfort and the Wausau Whatzit). If they are all just different views of the same, shape-shifting entity, then that neatly explains why Bigfoot corpses are never found and why they are so hard to catch.

The 2010 Tree-Liner

A Jefferson County woman reported one of the state's most recent sightings shortly before the deadline for this book. Strangely, she is a granddaughter of a man, Mark Schackelman, who saw an upright, furry creature digging on an Indian mound near a St. Coletta home for developmentally disabled people in 1936.

"I had always questioned that story of his," she said, "but now I'm a believer."

The fifty-one-year-old woman had never experienced anything really strange in her life before, she said, but on July 15, 2010, she was driving east on State Highway 106 when that secure outlook changed for good. She looked to her right at a spot along Jaeckel Road and saw a figure covered in dark fur standing near the tree line twenty to thirty feet away. She estimated it stood at least six feet tall and weighed 250 pounds or more. It was covered with black fur, except for a grayish area around its stomach. Its head, which she said seemed too small for its body, was bent as if it was trying to hunch over to make itself less conspicuous. As she watched, it turned and swiftly melted into the small stand of old pines and brush.

The creature's legs were like a gorilla's, she said, and its long arms hung down at its sides. It kept its head bowed down as it ducked for cover so that she never got a good look at its facial features. She did not see a tail when the creature's back was toward her.

"My head was just trying to process what it was," she said. She pulled the car over and stopped with the front passenger window rolled down for about one minute, but did not see or smell anything. She could not leave the vehicle to investigate, because she had a small child in the backseat, but she did return the next day for another look, also fruitless.

She said she was on that highway because she was interested in buying a house in the area, but is now afraid to live there. The house, a remodeled school with an old cemetery hidden behind it, had a hole in the aging foundation that looked to her as if it might have been dug by some large creature. She could not help but wonder if the hole's digger was the same big creature she saw only a few miles west of the house.

The sighting spot is also only a few miles west of the Hebron area, where Andy Hurd saw a Bigfoot in 1993, and is quite close to the Bark River, where a fisherman saw a bipedal, hairy hominid on shore in 1980. Highway 106 is the road where teenaged witnesses Tom Brichta and Chris Maxwell said they saw an upright canine in 1992. It is also not far from the Palmyra area, home of the Bluff Monster. The stand of trees where the 2010 witness saw the creature hides a small farm with fields and cornfields behind it that eventually lead south to the Bark River.

I'd say the possibility of the creature being a hoaxer in a gorilla suit is unlikely given that the incident happened in broad daylight in the middle of a very hot July day. And a bear—a rare sight this far south in Wisconsin but not impossible—would have been loping away on all fours.

The woman, who asked to remain anonymous, said the tall, dark creature was like nothing she had ever seen. I tend to believe that. If she had been copycatting her grandfather's sighting, I would have expected her description to sound more like his, with prominent ears, a canine head, and a different body structure. His sighting was also famous for his assertion that what he saw gave a growl that sounded like a primitive word that he interpreted as "Gadara." His granddaughter heard no sound from the creature she saw.

Could the animal the woman saw have been the same thing that her grandfather encountered in 1936, despite the differences in appearance between the two creatures? If so, the big hominoid would be well over seven decades in age, and there is no real reason to connect the two other than the odd coincidence of her relationship to Schackelman. But maybe that explains the gray belly area. I'm sure that she wishes her grandfather was still here to compare notes.

Creatures of the Sky

M onsters, it seems, inhabit every sphere of earthly existence —land, water, and sky—as do our known landlubber mammals, birds, and fish. That is a good thing to keep in mind when looking for unknown fauna, because some of them might otherwise go right over your head: dragons, giant birds, bats with humanoid bodies—all of these belong to the air above us. Unfortunately for a few human observers, the winged things also sometimes land.

And as usual, Native Americans knew all about them before the first Europeans arrived.

One of my favorite images comes from the famous Chief Black Hawk, leader of the Sauk and Fox people in the infamous war named after him. Writer Michael Edmonds, in an article in the Spring 2000 *Wisconsin Magazine of History*, cites a 1932 biography of Black Hawk in which the chieftain tells of a "good spirit" that protected Rock Island in the Mississippi River south of the Wisconsin-Illinois border. The spirit lived in a rock cave there and often showed itself to the Sauk people. Black Hawk, who was born on the island, described the spirit as "white, with large wings like a swan's but ten times larger."

Since a normal swan's wingspan is six to eight feet, we are talking one large spirit bird! Edmonds noted that indigenous people considered large birds such as cranes or hawks that could fly above the human range of vision to be excellent messengers to the spirit world. They also saw the birds as spirit guardians or protectors.

A better-known mythic Native American avian was the Thunderbird, whose huge wings caused thunder booms and whose eyes sent forth bolts of lightning. These creatures fought water monsters and figure prominently in the pictographs, effigy mounds, and other artwork preserved from ancient times in Wisconsin.

Many of the flying creatures seen in modern times seem to show a darker side, however. Whether the influx of new people and cultures introduced a more diverse aerial pantheon or some unknown portal from a scarier land has set other things free to fly, people have reported airborne oddities statewide. Some appear nasty enough that we could probably use one of Black Hawk's giant, white, good spirit birds again.

Dragons of Green Bay

Most people think of dragons as completely mythical creatures, scaly refugees from medieval fairy tales and Chinese folklore. But on October 27, 2007, a group of people in Oconto Falls saw something in the sky they described as looking like nothing other than those legendary flying reptiles.

A man named Sean had attended a concert of local bands at a downtown arcade. Sean joined a post-concert jam session and then the group gathered outside to "hang out," although the weather was cold and partly cloudy. As they talked, one young man thought he saw something odd in the sky. The others kidded him, but having nothing better to do, they all laid down either on the grass or atop their cars and watched the dark sky.

Sean wrote that "after about fifteen minutes of talking and laughter, those emotions changed to surprise as we watched a massive, tan and white dragon fly over the clouds."

The creature was almost silent as it flew and appeared larger than an airplane. It had a prominent tail, leathery or bat-like wings, a long neck, a narrow pointed head, and scales that cast a dim reflection of the streetlights below, said Sean.

The group decided they must have had some sort of mass hallucination, but then the creature came flying back over them, headed in the opposite direction this time.

Some of the group were from Green Bay and needed to leave to get home on time, but Sean and a female friend went to his house and watched the sky from the backyard along with Sean's mother. His mother did not believe him, he said, until another of the creatures flew over them. He wrote that her exact words were:

"I'm tired and I'm going to bed; I doubt that it even—holy [expletive]!"

They kept watching and were rewarded with the sight of a few smaller ones that night. No more of the scaly fliers have shown up in the skies over Oconto Falls since then, as far as he knows, although he met one person who had claimed to have seen them two years earlier.

The description sounds much like that of a pterosaur, one of a group of flying lizards that could attain up to a forty-foot wingspan and died out around the end of the Cretaceous era.

Perhaps some surviving relic of the pterosaur family inspired the first dragon tales told by our ancestors. In a guest spot on my *Wereblog* at beastofbrayroad.com, Richard Freeman, Zoological Director of the Centre for Fortean Zoology, posted this on March 28, 2009:

Forget demons, werewolves, giants and vampires; the dragon is the most ancient, powerful and widespread of all monsters. It is found in every culture reaching back 25,000 years. No other beast has such a hold on the psyche of mankind. In the west we associate the dragon with fire but worldwide it is more associated with the element of water. Dragons were intimately linked with and had power over water. In most cultures they were associated with fertility and life. . . . Dragon sightings are still reported today.

Freeman then related another sighting that occurred in San Francisco Bay in 1985, when two brothers saw a strange, black creature chase a sea lion out of the water. It was covered in scales that ranged from black to green to yellow-green on the underbelly and had serrated green "fins" that looked like wings. The witnesses estimated its length at over twenty feet.

Perhaps those Oconto Falls dragons were on their way to 'Frisco, too. The weather there is certainly better for reptiles.

Jurassic Skies: Twenty-First-Century Pterosaurs

Wisconsinites have spotted oversized birds that sometimes resemble pterosaurs all around the state for years. The book *Weird Wisconsin*, which I co-authored with Richard D. Hendricks, cites several prime examples.

One happened in Brookfield, a suburb of Milwaukee, in September 1988, as a man stood inside the Elmbrook Memorial Hospital, gazing through a large window at the sky. The hospital is situated in a surprisingly rustic area, and the man, a visitor to the facility, was enjoying the view over an adjacent bluff when something birdlike but bigger than a pickup truck dived down through the clouds and came gliding straight for him.

He estimated its wingspan at over a dozen feet and was shocked when it came close enough for him to realize that its surface was leathery, not feathery. Its long beak and narrow, crested head reminded him of a pterodactyl, a type of pterosaur familiar to prehistoric creature buffs. Although he was somewhat afraid that the big bird might try to dive through the window at him, the creature appeared to lose interest and zoomed back out of sight.

Jefferson County and Mauston Big Birds

Another big avian cryptid dubbed the Mauston Birdman sounds a lot like the popular Muppet named Big Bird from TV's *Sesame Street*.

In 1980, a ten-year-old girl who lived on a bluff five miles west of Mauston heard screams coming from the trailer next to her family's house. The screamer was her grandmother, who lived in the trailer, and she was yelling that she had seen a "bird man." It was broad daylight. The grandmother said the creature had a long beak, yellow feathers, and stood six feet tall as it peered into the kitchen window at her.

The grandmother was able to see the creature's whole, strange body and noted that its legs were like a human's, except for big, birdlike feet with talons. There was no mention of whether she saw it fly away.

Strangely, the ten-year-old's younger sister had insisted a few years earlier that "Big Bird" had come to play with her at night, but the story was dismissed as childish imagination.

A similar Big Bird–type entity appeared to a young woman and her boyfriend in Jefferson County on State Highway 18 near Paradise Road. This highway borders the Jefferson Marsh and has a local reputation as a spook lane.

The tall, humanoid bird man stood at the side of the road looking back at the pair with glowing red eyes. It was equipped with huge, dark, feathered wings at its sides and had a face the observers thought was "demon-like." It does indeed sound like an ostrich from hell. The couple was too creeped out to investigate. Understandably, they just kept driving. This incident was described in *Hunting the American Werewolf* and originally appeared on the *Weird Wisconsin* website.

Flying Lizard Men

There are witnesses and there are witnesses. Whether it's fair or not, some people who see strange things are judged more credible than others. Wearing an official uniform seems to help, and being part of a large group that simultaneously saw the same thing also boosts the believability factor.

The Medford Lizard Man flap boasts both of these desirable eyewitness characteristics, which makes this an incident that is very hard to explain away.

No less important an official than a warden with Wisconsin's Department of Natural Resources (DNR) was headed up State Highway 13 south of Medford one day in the mid-1990s when he spied something that was not found in any of his guides to Wisconsin animals. Standing smack in the middle of the road ahead of him was a humanoid, reptilian figure the size of a man—but covered with green scales.

The warden bravely continued driving toward it, but before he came close enough to hit the creature, it unfolded two wings that apparently had lain hidden behind its back and shot up, up, and away—over the warden's vehicle. Not finished toying with its human observer, the creature then landed on the road behind the car. The warden did not stop to see what would happen next.

This encounter might have been seen as a mere hallucination of a road-weary state employee had not a truck full of highway employees spotted exactly the same enigmatic lizard man near the same spot on the highway, not long after the warden's encounter. Again, the unknown creature spread its leathery wings and took to the sky as the men approached, this time disappearing into a patch of trees.

Not far from that highway runs the Black River, which can be followed southwest all the way to where it joins the Wisconsin and Mississippi Rivers at La Crosse. This seems to be a popular route for crypto-creatures, as the next story will attest.

Man Bat of La Crosse

Chiroptophobia, or the fear of bats, is a fairly common psychological trait. Even though most bats are small, timid creatures, something about those leathery wings and tiny fangs seems to trip our self-preservation alarms. Tales of vampires and myths about bats getting wound up in people's hair do not help the reputations of these helpful, sonar-enhanced flying mammals.

Imagine then the shock and surprise of two La Crosse–area men who found themselves staring into the hairy, fanged face of what looked like a bat with a ten-foot wingspan!

The two musicians, a man in his fifties who goes by the Cherokee name of Wohali and his twenty-five-year-old son, were returning from a band practice session in La Crosse between 9:15 and 9:30 P.M. the evening of September 26, 2006. As they ascended the hill on Briggs Road west of Holmen, something huge flew at their windshield. It was a humanoid figure around six feet tall, covered in fur but with visible ribs. It displayed a snarling, open mouth, fronted with big, sharp teeth. Its clawed upper limbs held bat-like wings that extended beyond the width of the men's pickup truck for a span of what Wohali estimated at ten feet or wider.

Just as the father and son were sure the creature was about to ram their windshield head-on, it shot straight upward and disappeared into some nearby trees, while emitting an ear-shredding scream that Wohali described as "terrifying" and unlike any sound he had ever heard in that area. That is saying a lot, because that locale borders the Mississippi Upper Valley Wildlife Refuge, a huge haven for all types of creatures. The section of Briggs Road where the incident occurred is not residential, with a shooting range to the east and a utility station adjacent to a wooded bramble on the west.

Wohali is not sure whether it was the shriek, the emotional shock, or some other unknown effect, but both he and his son became physically ill, with his son needing to pull over and vomit on the way home. Neither had been drinking alcohol or using drugs of any kind, he said. The flu-like sickness lingered for several days for the son, longer for Wohali. The same kind of illness has sometimes been reported by people who see other types of unknown entities. Vomiting and flu-like illnesses are also consistent with exposure to extreme ranges of infrasound and ultrasound, sounds at wavelengths either too low or too high to register in the human ear.

In the days and weeks following the sighting, the pair felt harassed by some unknown entity at their rural home. The doorknob would shake and rattle, there would be pounding on the door and walls, and the family's dogs would quake under the furniture, but neither Wohali nor his son ever observed anything unusual when they would peer outside. This gave them the feeling that perhaps the creature they saw was something from the supernatural world.

This sighting of a winged humanoid reminds many of the famous Mothman appearances around Point Pleasant, West Virginia, in the 1960s, documented in the book *The Mothman*

Prophecies by researcher John Keel. In one of the first sightings, in 1961, the Mothman also shot straight up in front of someone driving near the Ohio River. The Mothman had a rather different appearance, however, than the La Crosse beast and was often described as having a neckless head and large, glowing red eyes, and resembling a huge bird more than a bat.

Many writers have interpreted the Mothman's appearance as a foretelling of doom, since on December 15, 1967, the Silver Bridge in the area of the sightings collapsed and killed forty-six people in the Ohio River. Strangely, Wohali's Man Bat appeared three days before the drowning of a male college student in the Mississippi River at La Crosse, part of a long string of similar, unexplained deaths.

At least two other witnesses have reported seeing something large and slithery in a backyard on French Island, a part of La Crosse, and there is also the strange lizard man mentioned above to add to the river town's odd menagerie.

Flying creatures have been considered messengers of the gods in many cultures. Point Pleasant had a prior experience with such a belief, as author Loren Coleman points out in his book *Mothman and Other Curious Creatures*. He cites researcher Mark Hall's discovery of a 1900s "folk tale" about a giant bird with a human-like head and a twelve-foot wingspan that seemed to always appear just before some horrific event in the Point Pleasant area. Hall theorized that the creature was actually a giant owl.

If Wohali's description had not included bat-like rather than bird-like wings, another large bird species might have provided an explanation for his experience. Naturalist John James Audubon documented the Washington eagle, a giant bird of prey with a ten-foot wingspan, as late as 1840. Moreover, another eyewitness sighted a huge bird that fit the big eagle's description near Stillwater, Minnesota, in 2004. Biologists believe the Washington eagle extinct, however, and the fact remains that it was a lot more feathery than the flying thing observed by Wohali and his son. Weirdly, "Wohali" means "eagle" in the Cherokee language.

There are still a few birds flying the planet's skies that can reach such sizes. In mid-August 2010, an escaped African bird called the Rueppell's griffon vulture caused a minor panic in Scotland. The female vulture named Gandalf was part of a daily show at the World of Wings Centre in Cumbernauld, and she normally takes a quick fly-around and then returns. This time, however, it appeared she was caught in an updraft as she disappeared beyond view. This was alarming for various reasons, not the least of which is that with a ten-and-a-half foot wingspan, Gandalf could knock out a small plane or copter. Authorities notified airports, as there was no way to tell where or how far she might have gone. And it is easy to see how any uninformed citizen might be terrified at the sight of her and wonder whether something prehistoric had indeed breached the time-travel barrier.

Happily, Gandalf returned to alight on a nearby telephone pole about a week later, very hungry but otherwise fine. It is probably safe to say she did not make it to Wisconsin. The incident shows, however, that such escapes can and do happen. It might be best to just keep looking up.

Out-of-Place Animals

One quality that can make an otherwise ordinary animal seem like some kind of monster is the element of surprise. A bat that flits suddenly through darkened rafters or a goat that charges unexpectedly with head and horns lowered can incite fear and shock as effectively as a snarling devil monkey encountered on a forest trail. Perhaps even more upsetting are animals that show up in places they should not. To spot a kangaroo in downtown Waukesha or a small monkey-like creature in an Elkhorn grocery store is to confront the fact that in an uncertain universe, things are not always as—or where—they should be. If it doesn't fit, it is frightening. Wisconsin has certainly always been part of that strange, lost animal parade.

Rooing the Day: The Great Waukesha Kanga-Flap

For reasons as unknown as their mode of intercontinental travel, kangaroos seem to be the champions of out-of-place animals. They turned up in a nationwide flurry of sightings around 1900, and again, notably, in Waukesha County in April

1978, when southeastern Wisconsin suddenly began to look like an urban version of the Australian outback.

It was a school bus driver named Patricia Wilcox who first laid wide-open eyeballs on the Aussie refugees. And yes, that was an intentional use of the plural. She watched in awe as not just one but two kangaroos suddenly bounded across busy Moreland Boulevard in front of her bus. The street was crowded with morning rush-hour motorists who wheeled, skidded, and veered in a stunning display of evasive driving skill to avoid hitting the pair. After all, a fully grown roo can stand five feet tall and weigh more than two hundred pounds—enough to cause a vehicle massive damage. One of the animals did get nicked despite everyone's best efforts, but it jumped away, apparently unhurt.

Wilcox noted that one of the kangaroos was larger than the other, but no one knew whether it was a mother and her joey, a male and female pair, or merely two road buddies. But only one of them showed up a week later in Pewaukee to surprise a family of three at their evening meal. The Haeselich clan spied the medium-sized animal watching them from about fifty feet outside their window, but it whirled and sped away when one of the humans approached.

In the days and weeks that followed, small, single roos were also spotted by a couple driving east of Waukesha on County Trunk A and a social worker south of Waukesha on State Highway 83. A man named Lance Nero spied a pair of hoppers near his Brookfield home, followed them, and found unusual tracks that were declared deer prints by jittery local authorities.

As word got out, the media and jokesters got busy. Waukesha-area taverns invented a cocktail in the kangaroo's honor, and Milwaukee TV stations covered a "kangaroo hunt" undertaken by fifty merry Wisconsinites equipped with nets and ropes in Pewaukee. The hunters were well lubricated with the product of Milwaukee's famous breweries, and they provided great TV fodder as they attempted to flush the animals out of hiding by beeping handheld horns. The hunt was unsuccessful except for the capture of a man dressed in a homemade kangaroo costume.

Two enterprising hoaxers incited the public's imagination to a higher pitch when they somehow spirited a taxidermy-preserved wallaby specimen from an area museum and took a Polaroid photo of it propped outdoors. The photo appeared authentic and national news outlets pounced on it, convincing many skeptics that the roo was real.

Other hoaxers jumped across county roads at night while hiding behind a life-sized plywood cutout of a kangaroo and were very lucky not to have stumbled and been run over by a panicked motorist. In the end, it became hard to know which kangaroo encounters were real and which were pranks or illusions manufactured by devious jokers.

Skeptics might be tempted to consider these hoaxes proof that no real kangaroos ever romped Wisconsin byways, except that a flesh-and-blood roo was actually caught alive on the state's western side several decades later.

Wild Western Roo Roundup

Startled witnesses began to claim sightings of a renegade kangaroo around Iowa County in the first days of January 2005. The normally desert-dwelling marsupial was evidently not fazed by frigid winter conditions, as numerous motorists spied it bounding around U.S. Highway 18/151, south of Dodgeville.

Iowa County sheriff's deputies thought at first that it might be a local escapee belonging to some exotic pet fancier. They called on area resident and wallaby owner Cheryl Martens to see if her mini-marsupial (wallabies are smaller than kangaroos) was on the loose, but Martens had sent her pet out of state for a romantic interlude. Intrigued and concerned for the animal's welfare, she joined deputies in the hunt. They did find the large, red-furred male close to where drivers had reported it, but could only look on helplessly as it made for the nearest woods and disappeared.

On Monday, January 3, the sheriff advised area residents not to approach the kangaroo if they saw it, reminding them that roos can be dangerous. Those big legs can pack quite a wallop, and the animals are not averse to biting humans, either. Deputies armed themselves with tranquilizers, hoping for a safe capture.

The puzzle of the fugitive's origin continued to grow as all area zoos avowed their own kangaroos were present and accounted for, and authorities could find no other private kangaroo owners. Animal experts became fearful that the loose kangaroo would soon succumb to western Wisconsin's bitterly low temperatures and lack of edible habitat. Area residents kept close tabs on the progress of the hunt, and nicknamed the wayward creature Roo.

The bizarre creature saga ended Wednesday, January 5, when Roo finally allowed a farmer to lure it into a rural Dodgeville horse barn with the promise of a few apples. After a month's quarantine, the Henry Vilas Zoo in Madison adopted the 150-pound creature. It is now a star zoo attraction and goes by the new name of Boomer. That happens to be what grown male kangaroos are called in Australia, but the name has a second, more special meaning in this particular case.

In Madison, the name "Rennebohm" is a very familiar one. Oscar Rennebohm, governor of Wisconsin from 1947 to 1951, had started a chain of drugstores bearing his name in the 1920s. A large Rennebohm's pharmacy, complete with soda fountain, was a beloved Capitol Square landmark for decades. The stores succeeded so well that Oscar was able to start a philanthropic organization, the Rennebohm Foundation, which helped fund the University of Wisconsin's School of Pharmacy. What has all this to do with a misplaced kangaroo? Oscar's position on the Rennebohm Foundation eventually passed to his nephew, Bob Rennebohm, who had played professional football for the Green Bay Packers and the Detroit Lions. Bob and his wife Jean helped found the American Family Children's Hospital through the foundation, and the hospital named its "special procedures" clinic, a site where children receive chemotherapy, after the couple. Bob and Jean, touched by the plights of the children treated there, decided to create a small book that could be distributed to each small patient as a gift. Casting about for a book subject, they had only to open the newspaper and read about the capture of the loose kangaroo just a few counties to the west.

Jean, a former kindergarten teacher, wrote *The Mysterious Kangaroo, It's Absolutely True*, a spiral-bound, illustrated book that includes not only the Dodgeville story but kangaroo factoids and tidbits from around the world. It is now given to every child admitted to the clinic. In addition, the Rennebohm Foundation donated money to the Henry Vilas Zoo to help build a children's playground, complete with a kangaroo sculpture. Both the statue and the Dodgeville kangaroo are named Boomer, which happens to have been the college and football nickname of Bob Rennebohm!

There is another odd and rather tragic coda to the Dodgeville kangaroo tale. Almost a year after Boomer's capture, on December 7, 2005, a different and less fortunate marsupial met its end in Juneau County when rural Mauston resident Ralph Hamm hit and killed it in his driveway. According to a *La Crosse Tribune* article by Rhonda Siebecker Rothe, the animal, evidently a wallaby, leaped directly into Hamm's path as he was leaving his property. He did not see it in time to stop. This was a much smaller animal than the one caught near Dodgeville—only fifty pounds—and despite its mortal wounds it did no damage to Hamm's truck. The shocked Hamm called the Department of Natural Resources, which had no ready answers for him since wallabies are not native to Wisconsin.

Hamm could see from numerous tracks and marks in the ground that the critter had been holed up in a culvert on his property, possibly for a few days. Newspapers published a photo of Hamm lifting up the dead animal, so there is no doubt that it was a wallaby and not a dog, deer, or coyote. Again, no one had any idea where this wanderer had come from. Mauston is about sixty miles straight north of Dodgeville as the kangaroo hops. Had the two marsupials gotten away together and the smaller of them somehow survived the Wisconsin wilds alone for a year?

The best guess authorities could come up with was that both animals somehow escaped or were released from transient vehicles and the owners found it more convenient not to identify themselves. I find it interesting that as in the earlier Waukesha incidents, people saw two animals of different sizes, even if the western Wisconsin creatures did make their appearances eleven months apart from one another. The state's kangaroo capers remain a crypto-mystery, then, and the two pairs of kangaroos lend the whole thing a baffling sense of symmetry, as well.

Wanderoos

Kangaroos have also been spotted, but never killed or captured, in other parts of the United States, as well. One of the oldest sightings in the U.S. occurred in 1899 in New Richmond, St. Croix County, only about fifteen miles south of a little town with the odd but apt name of Wanderoos. A woman named Mrs. Glover insisted she saw a kangaroo bound through the property of her neighbor on June 12. There were two unusual circumstances in New Richmond that day. First, there was a storm with very strong winds, and second, a circus was in town. The circus, however, did not have a kangaroo in its menagerie. Could the animal have blown into town with the summer winds? Tornados have done stranger things. It may be noteworthy that New Richmond is also on the same side of the state as Mauston and Dodgeville, although it sits farther north.

Or perhaps the point of origin for sojourning kangaroos lies to Wisconsin's south, on the north side of Chicago. In October 1974, two Chicago police officers responded to a call from a resident who claimed a kangaroo was lounging on his front porch. Probably expecting the animal to be a misidentified dog or cat, the officers were confounded to discover the caller did indeed know his marsupials from his domestic pets. The officers chased the animal and tried to put it in handcuffs, but the boomer did not go gently.

In its best boxing-ring style, the roo leaned back on its tail and delivered a series of hard kicks to its would-be captors as the officers flailed back to no effect. The animal was able to leap away and lose itself in the city before reinforcements could arrive.

Author Jerry D. Coleman revealed his own Illinois brush with an escaped wallaby a good twenty years after the Chicago roo debacle in his book, *Strange Highways*. Not too surprisingly, his story had a strange Wisconsin connection.

Coleman was driving through South Barrington, Illinois, in early October of 1994, he said, when he noticed a hubbub surrounding Goebbert's Pumpkin Farm, a bucolic enterprise that featured a petting zoo. But instead of seeing children lined up to ride ponies, Coleman noticed groups of people brandishing sticks and combing the nearby fields as if searching for something. When he stopped to ask what was happening, he learned the farm's pet wallaby was on the loose.

The wallaby spent several days lunching at will in neighboring cornfields before farm employees captured it.

The Badger State link in this happy outcome is that the wallaby was on loan to the petting zoo from an exotic animal dealer named Mark Schoebel, who owns a farm called the R-Zoo in Neshkoro, Marquette County, Wisconsin. That is about thirty miles west of Oshkosh, not really close to either Waukesha or Dodgeville. But as it turned out, wallabies are not the only exotic animals kept by Schoebel, nor are they the only species to have escaped from his property.

A Siberian or Eurasian lynx got away from Schoebel's animal handlers as it was being moved to a new location in December 2008. The Siberian lynx is twice the size of the North American lynx, and males can weigh almost fifty pounds. It skulked near homes around Wisconsin Dells for a short time before the crew recaptured it.

This incident has led animal welfare groups to wonder what might happen if Schoebel, who also breeds and traffics in black bears and other animals, had an accident while moving one of his best-known exotics—white tigers—to a magic show at Chula Vista Resort. According to Schoebel in a February 2010 article on Madison TV channel WKOW's site, the tigers get around in double-locked "lion crates," but nothing is foolproof. If such a problem were to occur, or has occurred in the past, perhaps it would spark a sightings flap of one of the following creatures.

Big Cat Cacophony

Cougars, mountain lions, or pumas. Whatever one chooses to call these great cats, they have been in very short supply around Wisconsin for the last century or so. Although there is evidence that they have started to move back—one young male tracked through Rock and Walworth Counties was ultimately shot and killed near downtown Chicago in April 2008—most modern-day sightings of these furtive felines are greeted with great skepticism by authorities. And when witnesses describe large cats with black coats, the skepticism usually turns to downright disbelief. But both the buff-colored and the spookier so-called black panthers roam parts of this state, say many witnesses. With their fearsome claws and fangs, these large carnivores feel like something much closer to monster status than does an out-of-place wallaby.

Back in 1839, cougars were still common enough that it took a fairly extraordinary incident to make the news. The Wisconsin Historical Society's *Odd Wisconsin Archive* records one such event that occurred near Prairie du Chien on the Mississippi River.

A man named John Fonda was traveling down the river with his family when his wife spotted a large animal on a nearby sandbar. The beast appeared to be a large "panther," as Fonda called it, and it seemed to be dragging something big with its paw. Fonda shot the big cat dead, and then went to inspect his prize. He was surprised to see that the great feline had been trying to dislodge a huge turtle that had clamped onto its paw like an iron trap. Fonda forgot about the panther and instead took the turtle, which he made into a delicious soup that lasted the family for days.

According to American big cat investigator John Lutz, every state east of the Mississippi contains "substantial populations" of big cats that could be termed "cougar, mountain lion, puma or black panther." Lutz, whose Eastern Puma Research Network tracks sightings by state, has collected over 15,000 reports of large, black, or tan felines since the early 1970s, according to the Network's website.

From Under the Big Top

One early big cat sighting shocked the little Rock County town of Evansville in September 1901, when a spotted leopard ravaged area farms for three days, killing cattle and sheep and keeping residents indoors. The cat's origin was never in doubt, however. It was an escapee from the circus owned by Col. George "Popcorn" Hall, who wintered his animals in Evansville.

Area residents soon revoked the eight-year-old leopard's liberty pass. A farmer and an armed posse of thirty men surrounded the leopard in a tree after the beast ate two of the farmer's sheep. The leopard reacted aggressively. It jumped down and gave the elderly farmer, a man named Hess, a bloody mauling before turning to attack a second man. That man, Walter Tullar, managed to shoot the animal at close range. Hall's prized leopard ended up as a rug.

Wisconsin Cougars

More recently, two canoeists were enjoying the water on Rice Lake north of Edgerton in June 2010, when they saw a giant, tawny-colored feline dash across a hill and leap into a tree. Kalen Marsden and Chad Lovelace, both of Milton, kept their eyes on the long-tailed creature as they passed the tree where it crouched. It yowled at them, they said, before jumping back down and disappearing into the brush.

About a month later, in July, Edgerton brother and sister Doug Graf and Kathy Rudnitzki called DNR officials to tell them that Graf had seen a very large tan cat run through the woods on their farm. Rudnitzki noticed that chickens had gone missing at the same time, and had heard unearthly screams outside at night. She also found huge animal tracks in her garden.

A DNR official examined photos of the garden tracks with surprising results. Strangely, although Graf was positive he had seen a feline, the tracks left were not those of a cat at all but some type of big canine. According to an article by Neil Johnson in the *Janesville Gazette*, DNR operations supervisor Don Bates pointed to claw points on the prints as proof, because cats walk with their claws sheathed. They could have been made by a large wolf, he added. (It's hard to know what to make of that, but see the werewolves chapter for some ideas.)

A similar situation occurred in late January 2009, when something killed a horse on a Watertown farm in Jefferson County. The horse was savagely attacked by a wild animal in its head and neck area, the hallmark of a cougar's preferred kill method. As on the Rudnitzki farm, however, the DNR said the big tracks the creature left behind were those of some kind of large canine. Of course, cougars cannot leave dog-like prints, but again, it's possible this "cougar sighting" and the one in Edgerton were both cases of mistaken identification.

Johnson noted in the same article that only four cougars have been officially confirmed and identified in the state since 2008, including the one previously mentioned that ended up dead in Chicago. The other confirmed Wisconsin locations were Lima Township, Dunn County, December 2009; Pepin County, June 2009; and Spooner, Burnett County, March 2009. Biologists believe these cougars are males migrating eastward from an established population in South Dakota that has proved a genetic match for the new Wisconsin cats.

Besides the known cougar species, though, there are the much more baffling black great cats, which seem to have been padding around the state for a very long time. Author Hartley H. T. Jackson referred to an 1884 journal claiming a "black panther" was shot near Gordon the previous winter in his well-researched book, *Mammals of Wisconsin*.

Zoologically speaking, black or melanistic big cats are not supposed to exist except in populations of South American jaguars or African and Asian leopards. Might one of those animals be likely to have been loose in Wisconsin in 1884? In that same year, I discovered, the above-mentioned circus owner, Colonel Hall, purchased a South American jaguar at an auction, so he certainly had one of those animals at that time. We know from his later leopard escape that Hall's animal containment methods were not completely secure. It also stands to reason that if Hall was able to obtain an imported jaguar at auction, perhaps other circus owners did too.

Black Phantom Cats

There does remain the remote possibility of a melanistic mountain lion appearing in the state. Mutations of hereditary characteristics occur in nature in every species, and I don't find it impossible to believe that a few North American cougars could be born with black fur.

Some also believe that the great black felines many people have sighted around the world are not true jaguars, leopards, or cougars, but some species born of another world. People in Great Britain have frequently sighted creatures they call phantom black cats in certain areas for decades. One of the most famous in modern times is the Beast of Exmoor.

People started seeing what looked like a black puma around Devonshire and the fields of Exmoor in the southwest corner of England in the 1970s. No one paid too much attention until 1983, when some predator killed more than one hundred sheep by ripping out their throats in the usual way great cats bring down a kill. Photographers captured a few blurry images of a large, dark, cat-like creature, but that was as close as anyone ever came to catching the beast. In 2009, a strange, black-furred creature washed up on the shore at North Devon and many folks hoped the mystery had been solved, but it turned out to be only the carcass of a seal. As far as anyone knows, the crafty cat is still at large. But England has no monopoly on phantom black cats. Mysterious felines have shown up closer to home and much more recently than the Beast of Exmoor.

A southern Wisconsin fantasy author, Stephen Sullivan, and his wife Kifflie Scott, each had a separate glimpse of something large, black, and slinky that fit the phantom black cat's modus operandi in July 2004, about five days apart. The couple lives in Kansasville in Racine County, near a huge recreation area with a lake in the center and acres of marsh. The park was originally an Air Force base and is riddled with underground tunnels that are now closed. Both the couple's sightings occurred very near this area, and between County Highway J and State Highway 75.

Sullivan and the couple's two children were returning home from Burlington after an evening baseball game when he noticed a creature dash across the road, just illuminated by his headlights. He described the animal as "pitch black" and very fast with a tail that stretched out as far as its long hind legs. Although he felt it was about the size of a German shepherd, the creature moved so quickly that Sullivan said he could not be positive about the animal's species. Both his children also caught a glimpse of the swift animal.

Kifflie Scott had a little better look at the beast a few nights later, although it was also dark out when she saw it. Again, it ran across the road in front of the car, dashing north. Scott was able to see its sleek, thin tail and smooth rump, and had the definite impression that it might be some kind of great cat. She also noted its utterly black coloration. Neither Sullivan nor Scott thought that it was a dog.

In the days that followed, a curious figure began to appear along the same roadways: a jogger dressed all in black, including a black knit cap, despite the hot, muggy temperatures of midsummer in Wisconsin. Figures dressed all in black are often seen near places where paranormal events have occurred. Called "black monks" in older times, because they often sported hooded robes, they are now usually referred to as men in black and wear more updated apparel.

As I noted in my book *The Beast of Bray Road*, author Paul Devereaux proposes in his *Haunted Land* that these black-clad people are what he calls "landscape spirits," entities that are part of a land-based spirit matrix that can appear in many guises. These guises are usually black in color and may include the phantom animals as well as the mysterious men in black that appear later, operating in concert for their own, unknown purposes.

Or perhaps the jogger was merely the black creature's owner, searching for his big, ebony pet. According to Sullivan and Scott, the creature was not seen again and the jogger soon was gone, too.

Big Al, the Out-of-Place Bighorn

Sheep, woolly grass-eaters whose meek herd mentality makes them possibly the least monster-like creature imaginable, would normally have a hard time frightening anyone. Only a bighorn ram on the lam and extremely out of place might begin to qualify for a spot in a book on monsters. Even then, it's an admitted stretch. But in the spring of 2005, the Walworth County community north of Elkhorn known as Tibbets found itself the center of a media storm as citizens began to spot an adult bighorn thundering around their farm fields. Bighorn sheep are not commonly seen in Wisconsin; they are most suited to the more rugged habitats of the nation's western states.

The first woman to report seeing the shy creature called a DNR agent, who confidently informed her she must be mistaken since Wisconsin has no bighorn sheep. But within the week, the agent saw it too as it ran across the road in front of his car. He tried to take a picture, he told me in a phone interview, but could not get his camera aimed before the galloping animal had become a mere pinpoint on the horizon. He did confirm that it was a bighorn of a type normally found in Colorado.

The ram, nicknamed Big Al by Tibbetts citizens, began to visit a barn owned by Alan Hayden (also nicknamed Big Al) for regular treats of hay and apples. Milwaukee TV camera crews were able to capture video footage of Al hoofing it through Hayden's field and even a nearby cemetery, and Big Al the Bighorn became a local media darling.

Big Al began to branch out in his forays, and over the space of a couple of months made regular trips into the city of Elkhorn, eight miles south of Tibbetts, visiting school athletic fields and other points of interest. The area animal shelter and other authorities tracked and pursued him with tranquilizer guns, but Big Al was able to flee them every time.

The authorities tried desperately to discover a responsible party, to no avail. No one could find a game farm, zoo, or any other business or individual missing a bighorn sheep, and the mystery of the out-of-place animal grew.

Finally, Big Al's great adventure was tragically cut short when a car hit and killed him on State Highway 67 south of Elkhorn. A local sporting goods store claimed the carcass for taxidermy purposes. How he arrived in the neighborhood of Tibbets one fine day has yet to be discovered.

Snake by the Lake

In 1983, a fifteen-year-old Lake Geneva girl was spending a carefree summer day with friends about five miles north of the resort town of Lake Geneva when she encountered something straight out of a Hollywood horror movie.

As Randi Hanson, her sister, and two other girls raced down a gravel road at about 11 A.M. on that sunny morning, Randi sped far ahead of the others, enjoying the all-out run. Her parents' secluded, eight-acre property off Jones Road included two ponds that her family used as swimming holes. Randi had just crested a hill between one of the ponds and a cut-away hillside when she saw something only five feet ahead of her that made her stop in her tracks. It was a gargantuan snake, as thick as her arm and longer than the width of the road. She estimated it measured between about fifteen and eighteen feet long.

Even considering the size of the reptile, Randi was instantly sure it was a garter snake, with its long yellow stripes and black body. She had often captured smaller garter snakes for pets, and her father was a biology teacher who had taught her about the local fauna. But she also knew garter snakes usually top out at about three feet. There was something about the huge size of this one that simply wasn't right.

She was so close to the giant thing that she was afraid she would trip if she stopped, so she took a deep breath, leaped over it, and kept running. For some reason, she didn't think to warn the others and in fact felt reluctant to tell anyone about it. When her friends and sister finally caught up to her, she asked nonchalantly whether they had seen any snakes. They had not, so she assumed it had slithered off the road by the time they reached that spot. She decided to keep the weird event to herself.

Randi has always wondered how a garter snake that size could have been there, and whether it had anything to do with the fact that their property bordered a natural bowl-shaped depression that had once held a prehistoric lake. A time-traveling reptile, perhaps? She added that it "scared the living daylights" out of her, and that the incident ended her hobby of chasing and picking up snakes.

Certain aspects of the sighting give it a rather mystical quality: the snake's impossible size, the way it lay directly in her path, the fact that the three others did not see it, and Randi's fondness for catching normal garter snakes. Together, these factors make the incident seem like some sort of message aimed at Randi.

Many Native American tribal traditions teach that each animal species has its own master spirit that can appear as a giant specimen of that animal. Perhaps this big serpent was the master spirit of garter snakes, blocking Randi's path as a way of asking her to stop catching its babies. If this was true, it worked! Besides, I find it much more appealing to believe that scenario rather than accept that there are fifteen-foot snakes—time travelers or not—slithering around Lake Geneva.

The Divine Reptile and Other Wisconsin Gators

A four-foot alligator may not be considered a monster, exactly, and in fact may make an extraordinary pet in the right circumstances. But one whose scales spell out "God" is something else entirely.

The gator was owned by Wisconsin home-remodeling contractor Michael Wilk, who was given the reptile in December 2005. It was midsummer of 2006 before Wilk noticed the holy graffiti displayed on his twelve-year-old pet's side. A Florida alligator biologist verified that the scale pattern appeared natural, according to a July 19, 2006 article by *Chicago Tribune* reporter Courtney Flynn.

Wilk had hoped to start an alligator farm, said the article, and was keeping the gator in a 450-gallon pond in the southern Wisconsin town with the rather ironic name of Salem. Wilk later opened a pet store in Racine called Aquatic Oddities that was shut down in 2009 for alleged mistreatment of animals. There was no mention in several *Kenosha News* articles as to whether the alligator, which literally had God on its side, survived.

Badger State Gators

The state has a long history of brushes with gators, despite the fact that Wisconsin is a very distant and tedious swim from Florida, or even North Carolina, which is as far north as alligators generally venture on their own. In 1892, long before alligators had become popular as pets, residents of Janesville discovered a gator—five-and-a-half feet long from snout to tail—lying on the shore of the Rock River. Unfortunately, the month was February and the cold-blooded reptile was quite frozen. That meant it may have been there for a while.

Although alligators were indeed rare in northern states in those days, the Janesville gator may have been a refugee from a circus. The Ringling Brothers advertised an "alligator show" and they did visit Janesville on August 20 of that year. In May 1891, they toured southern Wisconsin. The Adam Forepaugh Circus came to Janesville in June 1891, and the great Barnum and Bailey show passed through southeastern Wisconsin and Chicago in late August and early September 1891. There was certainly some opportunity for a determined but climate-ignorant gator to slither off on its own, I think.

More recent sightings are likely to be cast-off pets that either escaped or became too big to handle. A reptile rescue operation in Jefferson County called the Serpent Sanctuary told Internet site *Channel3000.com* in June 2010 that it could not handle the number of unwanted alligators it was being asked to take in. One gator the sanctuary did take in, named Wally, had been left in an apartment in Rock County. Two others, both six feet long, had been living in the heart of Madison. The owner of the sanctuary said people can find alligators for sale online for as little as $25. The trouble is that the gators, like any living animal, tend to grow.

That is probably why Ed Long found himself staring into the reptilian eyeballs of a four-foot gator while duck hunting on the Milwaukee River in Washington County in late September 2007. Long instinctively fired and shot the animal in the head, killing it. The twenty-five-pound gator retained the ability to thrash reflexively even after it was dead, giving a couple of Long's relatives a bit of a scare, said *Milwaukee Journal Sentinel* reporter Johnson Johnson.

Long contacted a game warden, who told him that he had done a good thing by getting a member of an invasive species out of a state waterway. Long's plans for the carcass, said Johnson, involved either having the beast mounted or making a fashionable belt from its skin.

Johnson also noted that Washington County has been the scene of previous gator sightings, including two other four-footers found in the Rubicon River in 2006. A smaller one shot by police in nearby Dodge County in October 2005 was found lounging next to the Rock River in Theresa.

The gator invasion shows no sign of abating. In September 2010, a fisherman spotted a three-foot gator sunning itself on the shore of Big Muskego Lake. He wisely called authorities for help. The creature had slipped back into the water by the time conservation coordinator Tom Zagar arrived, so Zagar and the angler tried casting a lure next to it; to their surprise, the reptile took the bait. Zagar turned it over to a Waukesha County animal shelter, saving it from the fate of that first frozen gator found in 1892.

People who want to see live gators in Wisconsin without risk of personal injury can travel to Alligator Alley in Wisconsin Dells. Here, visitors may fork over moola to drop a live mouse or rat down a tube and then watch the gators chomp away on it. That experience may be enough to make people realize that a flesh-eating creature with seventy-four to eighty sharp teeth really does make a monster of a pet.

The Janesville Lizard

Janesville, otherwise known as the City of Parks for its many green spaces and scenic Rock River shores, was also known for a few weeks in October 2010 as the City of the Lizard—escaped lizard, that is. The four-to-five-foot-long, black-throated monitor lizard kept the whole city in a tizzy as citizens watched to see where it would turn up next.

First to spot the dusky-gray reptile was resident Amber Downing, who wandered outside her home at 613 Williams Street on September 28 to see what was causing her dogs to bark excitedly. She had left a terrier and a poodle in her backyard and was stunned to find that the pups had been yapping in terror as they faced down a huge, fork-tongued reptile. The creature stood hissing at the pooches in what seemed like a threatening way, especially since the lizard was bigger than both dogs put together. Downing scooped up her pets and dashed back indoors with them, and then she called 911.

Needless to say, monitor lizards are not native to Wisconsin. They come from various parts of Asia and Africa and require much more warmth than the average October temperatures of midwestern America can provide. Local animal experts quickly concluded that the animal Downing described to them was an escaped or abandoned pet, and that its chances for survival, especially in a week with nighttime lows dipping into the low 30s, were not good unless the creature could be captured.

Authorities had another pressing reason for wanting the lizard caught: large monitor lizards can be dangerous. They are meat-eating predators, and in the wild they will eat insects, birds, fish, mammals, or whatever they can catch and then gulp down in one piece. The beast in Downing's backyard may well have been planning to dine on her conveniently sized poodle.

And even though the lizard could not swallow a grown human whole, it might have inflicted a nasty bite upon Downing had she ventured too close. Larger monitor lizards can behave aggressively, and a bite can require stitches and intensive antibiotic treatment. Their teeth and viselike jaws are made for crunching small animals to death and can wreak great havoc on human arms or legs. On top of that, they may carry bacteria that can make bite wounds heal very slowly. Animal experts, however, noted that the Janesville creature's danger to humans was lessened considerably by the low outdoor temperatures that were sure to have slowed its metabolism and movements.

At any rate, the reptile hunt was on. The lizard escaped Downing's yard by slinking under a fence and into a neighbor's yard. It was spotted later that evening near Hyatt and Thomas Streets in the headlights of a motorist's car as the creature crossed the street and then slithered down a sewer drain. The drain, dark and probably warmer than the cool air above, would prove a good hidey-hole.

Three days after the first sightings, the *Janesville Gazette*'s Shelly Birkelo reported "Large Lizard is Still on the Loose." No other citizens had seen the creature, despite the fact that city police officers armed with dog snares had been scouring the area around Downing's house.

The break came about a week later at 5:46 P.M. on October 7, when area temperatures grew unseasonably warm and the sewer probably felt much less appealing to the lizard. It showed up back at Amber Downing's house, perhaps looking for another showdown with her dogs. Officers were able to nab the Janesville Lizard with a simple dog snare, and then turned it over to the Rock County Humane Society. The society, in turn, left the reptile with the specialty shelter in Fort Atkinson, Serpent Sanctuary, whose owners named the lizard Peter Pan.

While the big lizard's adventure sounds bizarre for Wisconsin, a county Humane Society worker told local reporters they have rescued as many as five of the creatures in a year. The animals normally either escape from owners or are set free when they become too large to handle. But Peter Pan is the largest to be caught in the county so far, according to the *Janesville Gazette*.

The area where the creature was first spotted and finally captured was only a few blocks away from Traxler Park and the Rock River, so it is possible that someone let it loose in the natural area on purpose. Police never found the creature's owners. If they had, the owners would have faced an almost $400 fine for keeping an illegal pet in the city of Janesville.

The capture was probably a matter of luck as much as anything. Monitor lizards are at home in the water, and even in captivity they require a water container large enough to serve as a bath. These reptiles are also very smart and have been observed to hunt in strategic teams. Experiments on captive monitor lizards have shown that the animals can even count! They also display the unsettling behavior of standing upright as if "monitoring" the situation around them. This trait was probably the source of their Arabic genus name, *Varanus*, which means "monitor" in English.

And as large as the sixty-pound Peter Pan must have looked to surprised Janesville residents, he actually falls somewhere in the middle size range of his kind; Nile monitor lizards, for instance, can reach seven feet in length. Komodo dragons can be even larger, up to ten feet in length and weighing 300 pounds.

These lizards are all thought closely related to some true monsters, aquatic creatures of the ancient seas called Mososaurs. Mososaurs bore a strong resemblance to Janesville's Peter Pan, but had flipper feet instead of claws, and they reached lengths of over fifty feet. Luckily they lived in the Cretaceous Age, so the good people of Janesville need not fear finding a Mososaur in their sewer system. Subterranean Janesville should be free and clear to shelter its next lizard on the lam.

Elkhorn's Weird Whatsit

Not all monsters are big and scary. Remember the classic *Star Trek* episode "The Trouble with Tribbles"? Small alien fuzzballs caused terror on the starship *Enterprise* by multiplying unstoppably. Sometimes, small and cuddly critters can cause just as much commotion as giant ones, especially when they come as a surprise.

Elkhorn, at the dead center of Walworth County, has developed something of a reputation for unknown and out-of-place animals. First there was that upright, wolf-like thing on Bray Road (see page 107). Then there was the rampaging bighorn sheep. But largely forgotten was a tiny beast that puzzled the town in 1939 after a produce vendor delivered a fresh shipment of bananas to a downtown grocery store.

The grocer discovered the small mammal hiding amid the banana bunches, but had no clue as to what it might be. The creature was about the size of a squirrel, but with huge, round eyes and a tail like that of a rat. It became known as the Whatsit and soon found a home with an area farmer named Adams.

It quickly became apparent that the Whatsit was a female, when she delivered two Whatsit young'uns one day. There is no record of what happened to the trio, or of any hint as to their true identity. This author's research shows they may have been a species of Central American rodent called a vesper rat (hence, the rat-like tail). In their native habitat, vesper rats live almost entirely in tropical fruit trees, so it is not likely that they thrived for very long on a cold Wisconsin dairy farm.

Hogs Wild

There is one other big animal making inroads into the Wisconsin countryside that remains almost universally unappreciated: the feral hog. Most people have heard of the famous eight-hundred-pounder from Georgia nicknamed Hogzilla that hogged the Internet in March 2005. But smaller versions of Hogzilla have popped up in at least twenty-nine Wisconsin counties (seventeen officially confirmed) all over the state, according to a story by Minnesota Public Radio. They are even making it just fine in the state's cold northern climes, with an estimated population of over one hundred in Douglas County in 2005. Wisconsin and Georgia's wild porkers are part of a bigger national problem, with an estimated four million at large in the United States.

These animals have earned their reputation as monsters by crowding out deer, gobbling pheasants and quail, spreading disease, wreaking havoc on sensitive water habitats, and snarfing up valuable farm crops. They are prolific, aggressive, and hard to trap, as well.

Douglas County resident John Loustari is waging war against the boarish intruders, according to the same MPR article mentioned above. At first he thought he'd been overrun with bears until he got a closer look and saw a herd of thirteen hogs—a breeding population! He called in the DNR, which dispatched agents with rifles to dispatch any pigs hungry enough to sample a pile of smelly, rotten corn. Actually, any citizen with a Wisconsin small game license can legally shoot feral hogs at any time—with no bag limit—but hunters can't seem to keep up with their burgeoning numbers.

WisconsinOutdoor.com told the tale of Eau Claire deer hunter Bobby Prueher, who picked off a deer in Clark County, but was shocked when the noise flushed four wild hogs out of the same brush. Prueher managed to down all four hogs, and had just finished the daunting task of loading all those carcasses when four more hogs came crashing out of the woods. He shot three of them. The site posted photos of his row of dark, bristly hog kills, and noted that game wardens congratulated him for his deed.

At least, no one is questioning the origins of these outrageous oinkers—they are not trans-dimensional or spectral entities. They were brought here from Europe and Asia by humans, starting with more than four dozen transported to New Hampshire from Germany in 1893 for hunting. Other wild boars came from Russia. Over the years, the animals spread across the country and some bred with domestic hogs to create hybrids.

Releasing feral hogs in Wisconsin is both illegal and unnecessary, because the hogs travel very capably on their own. In 2002, however, a Texas man named Robert Scott Johnson, who owned an elk game farm near Gays Mills, allegedly let thirty more of the omnivorous creatures loose in Crawford County. That's a heinous crime in any game warden or landowner's book, and Johnson was prosecuted for the act.

Before shooting feral hogs, it is a good idea to know what they look like. Feral hogs are usually dark in color, but there is no set description that applies to all of them. Their varied genetic history means the feral hogs can sport almost any color hair from white to red to black and all shades in between, plus spots and stripes. Boars can weigh four hundred pounds or more and sport five-to-eight-inch tusks. But neither feral boars nor sows have twisty tails like their farm brethren.

Their one positive attribute may be the fact that some sportsmen do like to hunt and eat them. That, in the end, may prove to be their downfall. Those who have dined on barbecued feral hog say that these destructive monsters are very, very tasty with the right sauce.

Shorties, Aliens, and Oddballs

Humans like to categorize and arrange things into neat lists that make it easier to understand what they are. That seems especially important, somehow, when it comes to a topic like monsters that we understand very little about. Even within this book, I have tried to group anomalous creatures into tidy and separate piles, with Bigfoot swept into one corner and huge flying things into another.

I find it vexing when something comes along that will not fit into the dustbin. This chapter may be considered the place for loose ends and nonconformists of the Wisconsin monster world. Some seem ghostly and supernatural. All of them are confounding.

Where do these things come from? The late researcher John Keel thought he knew. In one of his columns for *FATE* magazine (October 1999), he wrote, "There is an entirely different universe beyond the odd little reality that our feeble human brains have constructed. Nothing is real there. Everything is energy." Keel believed that sometimes, a denizen of that other universe can "alter his energy vibrations or transmogrify" in order to become visible in our world. Since there are no limitations on the forms pure energy can take, an otherworldly denizen might appear as a very weird creature to human eyes.

I will begin with one of the strangest: a "watcher" type of being that doesn't look like anything I've heard of before. It may make you want to check your own living room window the next time you pull into your driveway.

Eau Claire Humanoids

A woman from Hawkins, a town set northwest of Eau Claire in a region of state parks and marshes, had been busy mowing the grass at a local cemetery one overcast morning in the 1970s when she decided it was time to head home. She looked at her watch and saw that it was 11:15. When she looked back up, she realized she was not alone in the graveyard.

A tall figure stood near some birches at the edge of the grass, its pale, blank face turned as if staring at her. The creature's body was very dark, and its head was large and white. The woman had the feeling it had been watching her as she worked. She estimated that they watched each other for about ten seconds, and then the creature turned to its right and "vanished into the air around the trees." Strangely, the woman did not feel frightened and did not tell anyone.

Things got weirder. Later that month the woman came home one evening when the rest of her family was out of town, and as she pulled into the driveway, she looked into her living room and saw another white-headed creature similar to the first—perhaps it was the same one—sitting there in one of her chairs. It got up and took a few steps, and then it vanished. This one was also tall but had an orange body.

The woman didn't really want to go inside, but she had been grocery shopping and her ice cream was melting. She finally entered the house and found the place empty. The rest of her evening was uneventful, she said, and she has not seen the creature again.

She wrote:

> Now it is 2007 and I still wonder what these two very similar figures were and where they came from. . . . For years I thought the black figure was a demon whom the Lord had allowed into my life to test my faith. I no longer think this way. Were they demons, space aliens or creatures from another dimension? I am also coming to believe that a portal opened in Hawkins and allowed these figures to come in. Is it still opened?

The figures this woman saw do seem unique, almost a combination of ghost, alien, and Bigfoot. I find it interesting that the first one appeared at a cemetery. The fact that the creatures could vanish makes them sound otherworldly, for sure.

It's Not Easy Being Green Humanoids

It is usually not a great idea to pick up hitchhikers in this day and age. In the carefree 1970s, however, "thumbing it" was much more common, especially in areas around universities.

Four UW–Whitewater students, all women, were returning to the campus after driving to a Milwaukee suburb to visit a sick friend, when they all spied a figure standing near the roadside. The figure was in a classic hitchhiker pose. But it was not a classic hitchhiker.

The girls did not even discuss picking him up; instead they each simultaneously hit the manual door locks. It wasn't just that they had about half their drive still to go, it was the fact that the hitchhiker was naked—and green. He was also bald, shorter than an average human, and had big eyes that stared at them as their car passed by.

One of the students twisted around to see what the green humanoid would do and was shocked to see it successfully flag down another car and climb in. By then, the four young women were proceeding back to campus as fast as they dared drive.

The person who volunteered this tale became a high school English teacher in northern Wisconsin and said that she still thinks and wonders about what the creature might have been.

Another middle-aged woman confided to me after a paranormal convention in Eau Claire that she had seen a green man in her grandmother's living room in that town when she was eight years old. The "shiny" man appeared in the room as she was busy examining a mantel clock on her grandmother's fireplace. The being stood there staring at her. Thinking she must be imagining it, she scrunched her eyes shut, but when she opened them it was still there.

Perhaps rather ominously, she does not remember exactly what happened next or where the green man went. But like the first woman, its image is seared in her memory.

Pint-Sized Bipeds of Winneconne and Lake Geneva

The Wiowash State Trail in Winnebago County is a bicycler's dream as it winds through a thirty-seven-acre nature preserve and along Lake Butte Des Mortes (Hill of Death) between Oshkosh and Winneconne. A pair of teenage riders took a day off to make the entire scenic ride in the early summer of 1990, and they saw something on that trail that will not be found in any guide to local wildlife.

One of the teens, Mike, is now a correctional facility worker, but he has no trouble remembering the events of that day. As they started off down the gravel trail, they began to notice rustling in the adjacent woods as if something was following them, but hiding from sight. As the noise grew louder, Mike turned and saw that the noisemaker had stepped out of the tree line and was running just behind them on its hind legs.

The creature was only three-and-a-half-feet tall and had a dog-like face and body, with a long snout and pointed ears. It held its forepaws out in front of it as it ran, and Mike could see that it was fully covered with smooth, dark fur. Its eyes seemed to glow, he added.

It did not seem afraid of the bicycling pair, and in fact almost seemed to be taunting them as it appeared to give chase, sprinting fast enough on its hind legs to keep up with their bikes as they pedaled at top speed. The animal finally broke away only after a farm dog they passed began to bark at the racing trio.

The two young bikers might have convinced themselves they were only imagining things if they had not encountered the beast a second time about a month later on July 3. They were on a different section of the trail this time, said Mike, when they saw it dart out, pick up some dead animal, and scoot back into the brush of a nearby field. Their friends ridiculed their story, but Mike said he knows to this day what he saw—and it looked like a miniature dogman.

Almost ten years later, a family much farther to the south in Lake Geneva saw what sounds like the exact same creature. It was not running along a rural trail but a very busy highway, State Route 50, which runs between Geneva Lake and Lake Como on its way from Delavan into the city of Lake Geneva. A forty-three-year-old man and his fifteen-year-old daughter saw something cross the highway at about 9 P.M. the night of Tuesday, January 26, 2010, where the highway intersects Schofield Road at the El Dorado subdivision, a little outside Lake Geneva.

The man and his daughter were just passing Wood Elementary School when the creature jumped up onto the shoulder of the south side of the highway and dashed across the road on its hind legs. The night was hazy but light, and the creature was fully lit by their headlights, so they got a good look at it.

The father described it as three to four feet tall, the same height as the Winneconne trail creature. It was also covered in long, black or dark brown fur and had a dog-like tail and pointed ears—definitely canine. It loped quickly across the road and then disappeared into a stand of woods.

The father felt that he finally had an explanation for the odd grunts and growls his family had been hearing at night in their nearby home. He wasn't much comforted.

While the short creature might have explained the night noises, I am not sure what can explain the size of the creature in either sighting. A coyote would stand about that high on two legs and so would many small domestic dogs. Neither of those canids, however, is normally any more disposed to run on its hind legs than is a wolf or any other four-footed mammal.

Female beavers have been observed to cross roads in an upright position while carrying their young, and in both mini-canine sightings there were lakes only a short distance away. A beaver, though, has a wider body and much shorter legs so that its walk resembles more of a waddle. It simply would not look like an upright canine.

That leaves me wondering if these bipedal pups are junior versions of something else entirely. Exactly what the senior version looks like will, again, be discussed later.

Little People of the Lakes

Dogs and wolves are not the only creatures to come mini-sized. Humans do too, according to our native people's lore.

The Ojibwe still revere a spot called Marble Point on Lake Superior. The jutting bit of land in Iron County, just north of Graveyard Creek, was named Marble Point by early white inhabitants who thought that the strange, perfectly rounded little rocks they found on the shore resembled the marbles their children played with.

The Ojibwe call them spirit stones and believe that within each round stone resides the spirit of one of the "Little People." Despite their size, the Little People were very powerful and would punish those who took deer or cut trees on their land.

Scientists call the spirit stones concretions and believe they were made 20,000 to 30,000 years ago from sandy clay by the motion of water on the bottom of Lake Superior. Some form conglomerations of little rounded mounds, giving them the appearance of tiny, plump humanoids.

Although the Bad River Chippewa now own all the land where the concretions are found, a former professor of philosophy named Byron Buckeridge once owned property close enough to that area to amass a collection of 50,000 spirit balls. He has exhibited some of the more exotically formed examples at several sites around Wisconsin.

James P. Leary in his book *Wisconsin Folklore* asked Ojibwe storyteller Dee Bainbridge of Ashland to shed some light on the Lake Superior Little People. She said, "They're supposed to be little miniature Indian people. They live at Waverly Beach. And during the thunderstorms, when it's lightning and thundering, they're busy making concretions." She added that the beach had once been considered a sacred place.

Leary interviewed another storyteller, Keith Wilmer, on the same topic. Wilmer said that his cousin had the ability to see Little People when he was between the ages of seven and fourteen. There were two kinds: "bad" ones, who scurried around his bedroom floor at night and tried to abduct him; and good ones, a woman and a man, who perched on his bedposts and acted as his personal guardians.

Stan Cuthand, commenting in a book on ancient Cree beliefs called *The Order of the Dreamed*, also discussed these Memekwesiwak, as the Algonquian-speaking tribes call the

Little People. He described them as "relatively benign and comical." Their preferred habitat is riverbanks and coulees. Cuthand said he knew a man who had seen one standing in a river and the sight made him shout out loud. By the time nearby bystanders turned to look, the little man had submerged and left only ripples in the water as proof he had been there.

Cuthand added that while the creatures are friendly to most humans, the Memekwesiwak enjoy playing pranks on people who do not believe in them.

He also described another small creature of the northern woods, the Pakackos. This is a four-foot-high, skeletal creature that once was a human who either froze or starved to death. It has long, icy fingers and comes equipped with a tiny rifle that can be heard making popping sounds when ice covers the trees. It is a sort of dwarf relative of a different entity, the full-sized, skeletal Pakahk, which also is the result of a starved human but becomes a helpful healer and hunting spirit with powers of flight. Believers offer Pakahk an animal bladder filled with melted fat—the most filling substance possible—at a yearly ceremony.

Little European Immigrants: Les Lutins and Leprechauns

Many of Green Bay's early residents were French, and they brought many of their traditions with them such as Les Lutins, little folk that generally lived in horse stables. Gard and Reetz's *Trail of the Serpent* relates one elderly French man's memories of the wee people.

"It is rather hard to describe Les Lutins for they are neither devils nor angels," the storyteller said. "They are very tiny men, only about a foot and a half high." The strangest aspect of their appearance was that they had only one eye, like miniature cyclopes. The neighborhood stable hand claimed that they wove and knotted horse tails at night and told area children not to touch the horse on mornings that its tail was found in that condition. If they did, he said, the little "goblins" would be able to get them.

The stable hand also said that he had actually seen one of Les Lutins poke its pointy cap up from a hole in the floorboards once when he stayed in the barn overnight.

France, of course, was not the only country to export tiny spirit people. Every year in March on St. Patrick's Day, images of leprechauns, mischievous wee folk of Ireland, can be seen everywhere. Most people believe that if real leprechauns exist, the little green-coated ones are far away, busily burying their pots of gold in the British Isles. But one family believed that a leprechaun lived in their rural home outside of East Troy in Walworth County.

Their story is told in *Strange Wisconsin* by a woman named Amy, who in the early 1990s was engaged to a man living with the family. Two young relatives aged six and eight also often stayed at the cozy farmhouse, and they began to mention to other family members that a strange, red-bearded little man was living in a wooden box in the kitchen. He was dressed shabbily and smoked a pipe. The children would often ask Amy if she could see him dancing a jig on the wooden table as they could, but none of the adults were able to make him out, no matter how hard they squinted.

The children also reported seeing an older man and woman, and Amy later learned that an elderly couple had died in the house years earlier, both on the same day. She didn't know if they were Irish, but perhaps the leprechaun had once belonged to them.

Between the Algonquian Little People, French Les Lutins, and Irish leprechauns, it appears the Badger State virtually teems with diminutive spirits. Wisconsin author Dennis Boyer offers his view of this unsettling state of affairs in *Giants in the Land: Folk Tales and Legends of Wisconsin*. Boyer believes that the Little People who guard the St. Croix River for the Ojibwe have met and married European wee ones, including not only leprechauns but the German poltergeist and Scottish bodach. He says the Little People's interactions can also be thought of as "cross-fertilization of folk tales."

This intermixing of mini-beings, says Boyer, has resulted in a cherubic new line of Little People that live in the area between Osceola and Danbury. Since they often inhabit bubbling springs, a good way to communicate with them is to whisper into the cracks between rocks near a spring, if you manage that without falling into the water. If the whisperer is lucky, the tiny beings just may burble back. It is up to the listener to translate their watery words.

Boyer adds that these spirits are not nice to humans who waste or pollute water.

Goat Man of Hubertus

Goat men seem to crop up regularly around all regions of this country. They bring to mind old images of Pan, satyrs, and the traditional figure of the horned, cloven-hoofed devil. Wisconsin has its own goat man legend, said to have originated around the days of the Civil War near Hubertus, a small community west of Germantown in Washington County.

As the story goes, a young bride and groom had set off for home one night by covered wagon and were lurching along on Hogsback Road when a wagon wheel hit a big rut and the axle splintered. The groom was no coward, having just returned from the war, so he set off confidently into the night to seek help. He told his bride that under no circumstances was she to leave the wagon, so she snuggled under some covers and settled in to wait. And wait.

She tried not to worry as the hours passed and still he did not come. She was just about to throw on her cloak and go after him when she heard what sounded like a wild beast pawing and sniffing the ground around the wagon. She peered out as best she could and saw what looked like a huge, hairy goat walking upright around the wagon as if planning an attack.

At that she decided to stay put, and lay frozen with fear for the rest of the night as the terrifying sounds continued. They finally ceased at sunrise, and she could see nothing to fear when she finally dared to poke her head out of the wagon. She followed her brave husband's trail of muddy footprints and cried aloud when she spotted his familiar jacket in the woods. But as she ran toward it, her joy turned to terror as she realized the jacket was covered with blood and the mauled body of her husband lay stashed in a nearby tree.

Local storytellers say that the goat man has updated its methods to accommodate modern transportation, luring unwary motorists to pull over on the steep grade of Hogsback Road so that they become stuck as fast as that Civil War–era wagon. Perhaps in this day of cell phones and GPS-guided locators, however, the goat man will have to become cleverer still in order to survive.

Other goat man legends can be found in Lancaster County, Pennsylvania, and Prince George's County, Maryland, to name a few. The goat men are almost never friendly.

Rooting for Pig Men

It is true that pigs share enough genetic code with humans that we can swap some swine parts, such as heart valves, for our own. But the idea of pig men existed before modern science discovered our handy biological compatibility, and they continue to live in lore and legend worldwide. They have even entered the realm of television sitcoms, such as the *Seinfeld* episode in which Kramer encounters a pig man in a hospital.

Wisconsin is no exception to the pigmania. At least three communities count pig people as part of their unofficial population, although confirmed numbers are hard to come by.

Marshfield is one such place. My investigation concluded that either this city has a few people who will believe anything, or a portion of its citizenry is very skilled at pretending that they do. Several different Marshfieldians told me with very straight faces that a clan of (literally) pig-headed people lived in a community just outside of town, and that they would often come to downtown Marshfield to shop at the Salvation Army store. The pig-heads were very frugal creatures. As proof that the creatures do exist, those citizens I interviewed pointed out a few tiny hoofprints made of black paint on the corner of the sidewalk in front of that store.

Perhaps it was those painted hoofprints that started the whole legend. One wag said the pig people were brought to town by a local politician who promised to bring home the pork. I have a feeling the legend's true originator is out there somewhere, having a few good snorts about the whole story.

Another blend of hog and human hails from Door County, an area fortified with a strong heritage of settlers from Brussels. These emigrants were a staunchly religious bunch and took such things as blessings and curses very seriously.

The pig men of Brussels were structured just the opposite of those in Marshfield, with porcine bodies and human faces. They are also much older, dating back to the time of the first settlers from Belgium, according to writer Esther Menn in her book *Wisconsin Footsteps*. Most of them were very devout Catholics. They built many little shrines and tiny chapels set in fields and at crossroads, both to provide places for worship and to ward off any stray evil spirits.

One farmer who was perhaps not quite so devout as his neighbors came to America with hopes of some day receiving a large inheritance from an uncle in the Old Country. He undoubtedly had great plans for the money in the new land of opportunity and eagerly awaited his uncle's demise—and the reading of the will.

Finally word came from relatives that the uncle had gone to meet his maker—and left his nephew out of the will entirely. Shaking his fist at God and the universe, the man vented his wrath by cursing the local priest. But the priest was so holy that the curse could not work upon him, so the evil intent returned to the one who had sent it. Or in other words, he who dealt it, felt it. The man's life became a living nightmare as his table and chairs danced around his kitchen to the tune of ghostly fiddlers and his horse grew a human head. And then the pig men—hogs with men's faces—began to follow him everywhere.

The man had gone nearly insane from the constant, menacing presence of the demonic manimals when a neighbor suggested he show repentance by building a shrine. He did, and the act of penitence worked. According to Esther Menn, the small, blue-and-white chapel sat near State Highway 57 for decades, until it was moved to an undisclosed location. As to where those pig men went, no one knows and no one wants to know.

There is one more noted pig man legend in the state, described by folklorist Dennis Boyer in *Giants in the Land: Folk Tales and Legends of Wisconsin*. Boyer calls it the Sprague Stumper Jumper. A woodsman in Necedah, Juneau County, claimed to have seen the half-man, half-pig critter lurking in the forest, dressed in shreds of old clothing. It survived by scavenging old hunting cabins. Rather than inspiring fear, locals admired it for assisting single women that needed a helping hoof. Those who saw the Stumper Jumper swore it had the ability to shape-shift from all man to a total pig.

It is probably safe to say that these tales of the three little pig men are not reports of actual creatures but true legends, whether folk or urban. As long as their stories are told, they may live on in our collective subconscious, rooting for corn or cookies and building their little chapels of brick and straw.

Hillsboro Hairless

Hillsboro is best known for its Czech and Slovak heritage, celebrated with a town festival every summer. But in 1992, a Hillsboro farmer puzzled Department of Natural Resources officials and caused a stir with his report of something that was decidedly not festive.

Ed Hora and his teenaged son Brian were tending to their usual chores when an unknown animal suddenly exploded out of a stack of hay and attacked their pet beagle. The intruder wasn't a large beast—only two feet long—but it was fierce. It did boast a prominent tail about nine inches in length, and weirdly, the beast was entirely hairless.

Hora swung a metal pipe at the creature until it finally gave up and ran away. The beagle escaped with its life. The farmer then dutifully reported the incident to local authorities.

DNR officials figured the hairless beast was probably a raccoon with a very bad case of sarcoptic or demodectic mange. This disease, introduced by the infestation of a tiny mite, can cause mammals to lose various degrees of fur, exposing gray-pink flesh and resulting in an agonizing itch—enough distress to drive any animal into attack mode.

In a similar vein, some people think that stories of a bloodthirsty creature called the Chupacabra or "goat-sucker," reported in Puerto Rico, Central America, and southern U.S. states such as Texas, have been inspired by sightings of coyotes made similarly bare naked by mange. Just such an incident occurred in Harrison Country, Texas, in March 2005, in fact. If there is such a connection between mange infestations and sightings of the Chupacabras, perhaps the Wisconsin beastie could be considered a mini-Chuppie. The little Hillsboro Hairless would make a great Czech festival mascot in any case.

Haunchies: The Legend of Muskego Lake

A decades-old legend centered around a Muskego street called Mystic Drive alleges that a colony of small, reclusive, and deadly small people nicknamed the Haunchies lies hidden at the end of a weedy lane. The Haunchies are thought to reside in a cluster of miniature buildings that they zealously guard from the prying eyes of outsiders. Those who even try to drive down the lane will be met by a shotgun-totin' normal-sized human in a black pickup truck. If the shotgun blasts fail to discourage the intruders, a determined horde of Haunchies will emerge from adjoining fields wielding tiny baseball bats. The intruders will next find themselves being beaten senseless, and then possibly hanged.

This full sequence of events happened to at least one man, whose image—in full hanged-man position—was burned onto the side of the barn where the execution occurred. The Haunchies could never be prosecuted because their acreage is riddled with underground escape tunnels. Or so the story goes.

Some have theorized that perhaps some actual little people once retired to this area from one of Wisconsin's many circus outfits, and their presence took on mythic proportions in the way that folk tales do. This author knows of one such colony of retired circus performers that lived discreetly on Delavan Lake in Walworth County for years.

Mystic Drive does contain one lot with several odd, tiny buildings, but they don't look like anyone ever lived in them. Besides, Haunchyville, as it is called, was supposed to be out of sight at the end of a long drive.

Searching for Haunchyville today is probably not a great idea. The street became such a popular destination for cruising teenagers that the police began issuing hefty fines to trespassers, and still do. Besides, the end of the street that once seemed so mysterious has recently been opened up for new housing development and roads. It is a sure bet that if the little people ever did live there, they have long since moved to someplace much more private. If so, I sincerely hope that this time no one will blow their cover.

As bizarre as this story may sound, there are similar tales from other parts of the country. Only the names for the little people are different. There are three such legendary locales in Maryland, named either Midgetville or Zoobieville. The grouchy inhabitants of these places are also guarded by a big guy in a truck, but the little people chuck rocks at trespassers instead of beating them with bats.

There is another place called Midgetville in Morris County, New Jersey, in a secluded forest near a former estate of circus mogul Alfred A. Ringling. *Weird New Jersey* authors Mark Moran and Mark Sceurman have documented a cluster of tiny homes they found at the site, each with entrances and windows too low to accommodate most grown humans. Hmmm . . . a circus owner nearby, little houses . . . it all starts to make sense. And I haven't even mentioned the Midgetvilles rumored to exist in Virginia, Kentucky, and Florida.

Like misery, mystery loves company, so perhaps Muskego citizens can take comfort knowing that whether the Haunchies exist or not, their city is part of a national trend.

The Furry Alien of Frederic

The ranks of those who believe aliens visit earth regularly seem to be growing, but there is great disagreement over just what the creatures seen peeking out windows in UFOs or hovering around a bedstead at midnight really are. Some think they are visitors from another planet, others believe they are fellow natives of earth that evolved underground. There is another theory that says the aliens are humans, visiting ourselves from the future—or even the past. Some believe they are demons in disguise, bent on the everlasting deception and destruction of our souls.

The creature that farmer Bill Bosak saw on his way home from an agricultural co-op meeting one night in early December 1974 might have been any of the above. But Bosak, sixty-nine at the time, decided that it must have been a being from outer space.

It was about 10:30 P.M., according to a newspaper article by Dewey Berscheid of the *Saint Paul Pioneer Press*, as Bosak crept along County Road W at thirty-five miles per hour about six miles east of Frederic in Polk County. The location was not far from the Wood River and a chain of marshy lakes, mostly lonely rural territory. Bosak was almost home when his headlights suddenly hit something bright and shiny sitting smack in the center of the westbound lane. This was a road that Bosak was extremely familiar with and therefore he knew this was something unusual, so he slowed down even more to see what it was that lay gleaming through the fog that had just begun to set in.

It was a vehicle of sorts, but like no other Bosak had ever seen. It was disk-shaped and had a transparent top made of what looked like curved glass, and inside was a creature looking back at him. Bosak could see the being from about the torso up, and noted that it was covered in tan fur except for its face. It stood with its arms inexplicably stretched upward and was humanoid in shape.

Its face, however, was unique. Bosak described it as square, with big, buggy eyes and long ears that stuck out horizontally from near the top of its head. He thought it stood "a little taller than a tall man." It also seemed afraid, and its pose had almost a pleading quality.

By the time Bosak had drawn his vehicle to a position only six feet away from the lighted vessel, his curiosity gave way to fear and he stepped on the gas, noticing a "whooshing sound" as his car passed through the strange vehicle's shadow. He was close enough to his house that he could look out a window and see the spot on the road where his encounter had taken place, but it was now too foggy to make out the object and he was scared to return in the dark. He said he did drive back the next day but the odd craft had not left any marks on the road.

It took him almost a month to work up the nerve to tell anyone. The local newspaper editor did not believe him, so he turned to the St. Paul paper. He told the reporter that he later wished he had stopped and tried to help whatever the creature was, and that the incident had made him a believer in UFOs.

W-Files author Jay Rath interviewed Bosak some years later, and the account in his book turns up one discrepancy from the *Pioneer Press* article. Bosak had told Berscheid that the craft was sitting on the road, in the other lane, and that it had made no marks. But he told Rath that he found a six-foot, round depression in a nearby hayfield the next day. Of course, the creature may have landed twice, but it seems odd that Bosak would have omitted such an important detail from his newspaper interview. Of course, Bosak was much older when Rath talked to him, and it's possible that the events became a bit muddled for him over time. But as for the craft and creature, Bosak said he would never forget them.

Perhaps the creature had an equally weird tale to tell its own folks about Bosak.

Lake Dwellers

One of Wisconsin's oldest and most commonly reported monsters is the lake serpent, a gargantuan, green, and slinky beast spotted everywhere from remote ponds to the shores of Lake Michigan. These sightings have been ongoing for more than two hundred years, even more than that if ancient native traditions of water panthers and big water snakes are included. Encounters range from quick glimpses of humps on the horizon to close-up views of a massive, open maw.

The prospects of actual large, unknown marine animals inhabiting Wisconsin's waterways may seem unlikely, but that does not stop people from swearing they have seen them. But before swimmers and boaters arm themselves with harpoons and depth charges, they should understand that the leviathan's portion of the sightings occurred in the past century or earlier. Lake monster sightings have definitely nose-dived over the last few decades. But perhaps that only means the state is overdue for a new crop of horrors in the water. Cue the theme from *Jaws* and keep a spare oar handy.

Rock Lake's Rocky

Some of the state's earliest lake creature sightings took place in Lake Mills in Jefferson County as early as 1869. The lake may be best known for its submerged, thirty-foot-high pyramidal stone formations whose origins—man-made or natural—are still hotly debated. The Native Americans living there at the time of European settlement called them rock tepees, but could not explain them. The mystery has never been solved to anyone's total satisfaction, partly because of the poor visibility in the lake's dark waters. But in the late 1800s, boaters and fishermen began reporting another mystery in Rock Lake's murk: a giant, snakelike creature longer than a rowboat seen snatching at their bait or lurking in the weeds.

The beast was no harmless phantom. One fisherman, Fred Seaver, said that it took his line and pulled his boat across the lake for about half a mile in its frenzy to escape. Another angler claimed to have actually speared it, but the beast was too strong for one puny human to drag to shore. He had to let it go. Alarmed people who lived around Lake Mills dubbed it "the Terror."

The creature seemed to grow more aggressive as the years passed, threatening two men racing each other in rowboats with an upraised head and open jaws lined with teeth. The men tried to fend the serpent off with their oars and were joined in their fight by some men on shore that hurriedly rowed out with a shotgun. The creature had disappeared by the time the rescuers reached the hysterical boaters, but it left a foul odor behind as a sign that something nasty had been there.

Sightings abated in Rock Lake as time went on, but strangely picked up again about five miles to the southwest in the smaller Red Cedar Lake near Cambridge in the early 1890s.

No one could explain how the water beast was able to transport itself from lake to lake, although it might have managed to swim through Lakes Hope and Ripley on its way. But by the time it was sighted in Red Cedar Lake, it had doubled in length to between forty and fifty feet and was sporting triangular-shaped back fins. Worse, it had developed a hearty appetite for landlubber farm animals and was said to slither into barns around the lake and drag livestock back into its watery lair, according to one farmer who saw it raid his pigpen. The creature left only pitiful remains of the stolen porker to wash back up on shore.

Where did the Slithery One go after that? Some think it skulked its way north, back to Rock Lake, where it evolved into the twentieth-century lake monster known as Rocky. Rocky showed itself in 1943 to Joseph Davis, a fifteen-year-old fisherman, who spied it from his rowboat. Davis only saw about six feet of it rise out of the water, but he said even that much told him the dark-brown monster was something he had never seen before. Although it hasn't been seen much since, today the creature has a beer—Tyranena Brewing Company's Rocky's Revenge Bourbon Brown—named after it, with its portrait on the label. By all accounts, the brew is as zesty as its namesake.

Long Lake's Long-Neck

Long Lake near Dundee in Fond du Lac County has a modern history of UFO sightings, starting in 1959, that has led the town to proclaim itself one of Wisconsin's three "UFO Capitals." (The other two are Elmwood and Belleville.) A nearby rise, Dundee Hill, was known to the area's indigenous people as Spirit Hill, and local farmers found a crop circle in nearby Jersey Flats in the late 1940s, before the world knew what crop circles were. With so much unexplained activity happening in this neck of the Kettle Moraine State Forest's Northern Unit, it would almost seem crazy if Long Lake did not have a lake monster to throw in the mix. But it does.

According to a letter from one Bob Kuehn published in the *Campbellsport News* on September 29, 1998, a woman told authorities the previous week that she had witnessed a strange, giant creature "undulating" its way through the lake only a few hundred feet from the shore. The lashing tail was powerful enough to generate waves higher than a nearby pier.

Kuehn added that five years earlier, a similar story told by five campers had made Milwaukee-area news, and that in 1984, two tourists told a store owner in Dundee that they had seen a dark brown, spotted, twenty-eight-foot, eel-like creature wriggling off the shore in Long Lake State Park.

The website *W-Files.com* posted the article in addition to a brief accounting of an interview with a Long Lake monster witness named Beth Quinn. Quinn was vacationing at the lake in 1994 when she saw something huge and black in the water with a swan-like neck but a "dragon-like face." She ran to bring other witnesses, but the creature had disappeared by the time they returned.

Monsters of Madison

Wisconsin's capital is hedged by its chain of four lakes: Mendota, Monona, Wingra, and Waubesa. The capitol building itself is set on the isthmus between Mendota and Monona. But according to witnesses, both ancient and modern, serpentine monsters snort and cavort around the lakes as if the Madison waters were no more than wave pools in a Wisconsin Dells water park.

The legends start with the ancient tradition of Winnebozho (spelling varies). He was the flesh-and-blood representation of the serpent god or "culture hero" of area Native Americans. They believed he caused waterspouts to appear over Mendota and overturned boats.

Fierce spirit animals called water panthers, or Mishepichoux (spelling varies greatly), also inhabited Mendota. The water panthers were huge, clawed entities with horned heads and were believed even after white settlement to inhabit an underwater den just off Mendota's north shore. The water panthers drowned both indigenous people and white settlers indiscriminately and did not limit their prowling to the north shore. Native people crossing the lake by canoe were always sure to sprinkle tobacco as an offering when passing through the most dangerous spots. Even looking upon one of these spirits, it was believed, could make a person go insane.

The chief business of the water panthers was to do battle with the great air spirits called Thunderbirds and thereby keep sky and water in balance and harmony. The water spirits and the Thunderbirds are well represented among the groups of animal-shaped effigy mounds left around Wisconsin by an unknown people between 800 B.C. and 1200 A.D.

As if the great serpent and the water spirit panthers were not enough for Mendota, a *Wisconsin Archaeologist* article by Dorothy Moulding Brown told of another fearsome fish thought to live there. This creature had a more unusual origin. It was originally a man who became a fish after committing a great taboo by eating a sacred raccoon. It lived in the waters off the now genteel neighborhood of Maple Bluff, and the Ho-Chunk who inhabited the area wisely left it quite alone. There is just no telling what a big fish that is part sacred raccoon might do to someone.

By the 1860s, Madison's settlement was well under way, and the lakes provided popular recreation opportunities just as they do now. But it wasn't long before the city's inhabitants realized their lakes provided additional thrills. Two of the first to figure this out were a man and his wife whose leisurely boat ride across Mendota was interrupted by a large, irritating brown log that suddenly blocked their way. The man used an oar to jab at the log, which proved to be a live, angry, and thrashing creature. The couple managed to escape.

Another early serpent spotter was a postman named Billy Dunn, and for a time the Madison lake creature was known as "Billy Dunn's Sea Serpent," regardless of the fact that Mendota was something less than a sea.

Thirty years after the initial sightings, two men witnessed a huge, eel-like creature swimming across nearby Lake Monona. Another man soon claimed the beast had tried to overturn his boat, and a dozen others said they had spied the long creature in the Yahara River that links the two lakes. A few sportsmen tried shooting the beast, but bullets were said to have no effect on the monster, and those who were able to eyeball its full length claimed it was at least sixty feet long. The creature was evidently carnivorous, as one report said it swallowed a dog (breed unknown) that was unfortunate enough to be caught paddling in the water. The great serpent was spotted in smaller Lake Waubesa, too.

Chad Lewis quotes an article titled "Lake Mendota Sea Serpent" from the August 4, 1899, edition of the *Racine Daily Journal* in his book, *Hidden Headlines of Wisconsin*, which describes one of the much-reported encounters. In part, it reads as follows:

It was seen this time by two women, instead of fishermen, as has always been the case in past years. Mrs. E. Grove and Mrs. J. J. Pecher and several other women . . . saw the serpent while they were out on a boat. They saw a long, snake-like monster with a head ten inches across and a tail which had horns. They started for shore and the serpent, apparently as much frightened as they, plunged, they say, into the depths of the lake, making a great deal of foam.

The Madison monster surfaced next in 1917, with eyes so bright they appeared on fire, said witnesses who saw it off Mendota's Picnic Point. It is interesting that one traditional, native "great water serpent," Mishegenabeg, was described in ancient lore as having large, shining eyes. The creature became something of a University of Wisconsin fraternity mascot, after it tasted a sunbathing student's feet with its tongue, and was known around campus as "Bozho."

It was also in 1917 that a student walking the beach found a curious object on Picnic Point's shore—a giant scale that a scientist at the University of Wisconsin could not ascribe to any known creature. Historian Charles E. Brown wrote about it in a 1942 paper for the Madison Folklore Society. He said that the science professor, who was from New England where sea serpents were much better known, believed it came from such a creature. "This was," Brown wrote, "so far as one can learn, the first well-verified indication that there was such a creature at large in the fairest of Madison's four lakes."

Jay Rath has tallied the Madison lake monster encounters and puts the total at a minimum of twenty-two witnesses who saw monstrous and unidentifiable water serpents in at least nine incidents.

Present-day lake traffic has increased from those early days, however, and Bozho and the water panther appear to have fled Madison waters. Perhaps they know how to navigate underground waterways to find more private swimming holes, or maybe they succumbed to old age. Or perhaps they crept eastward to the freedom and great depths of the Great Lakes, where waterspouts still rise and battles between water and sky rage unabated.

Lake Geneva's Jennie

About the same time as the Madison sightings, tourists and residents of Walworth County's Geneva Lake were having their own tussles with unknown lake titans. The second-deepest lake in Wisconsin, Geneva is kept crisp, cold, and clear by the underground springs that feed its eight-and-a-half square miles of water.

Like Madison's four lakes, Geneva has a long history of monster stories, starting with the effigy mound shaped like a long-tailed water panther that once adorned the shore of Flat-iron Park in the adjacent city of Lake Geneva. The Potawatomi who lived around the lake when white settlers arrived also believed that a jutting tongue of shore called Conference Point was the site of great battles between Thunderbirds and water panthers. The waters off this point are the deepest part of the lake. Conference Point is now home to a private religious retreat and author Gerald Lishka believed it to be the site of mystical happenings that he recounts in his book, *Darkness is Light Enough.*

The Potawatomi also said the lake was home to a massive, "eel-like" creature, said local historian Paul Jenkins in his privately printed *History and Indian Remains of Lake Geneva and Lake Como.* This creature was probably the same Mishebenegeg mentioned in the previous story.

The indigenous inhabitants of Geneva Lake evidently knew what they were talking about.

Three fishermen angling for their dinners in July 1892 were the first known people to see a great water serpent on Geneva Lake in more modern times. Ed Fay and two boys had just called it quits for the day when a massive, reptilian head splashed upward from the lake on a ten-foot-long neck and opened its toothy jaws wide in their direction. They said the beast was covered with brown scales that changed to pale green on its underside and that its round body had to measure at least three feet thick.

Naturally, the trio began to row away from the menace, but they had evidently piqued its interest, because it began to swim after their boat. Fay and the boys rowed for their lives, and were relieved when the beast lost interest and slithered away toward the mansion now known as Black Point. Interestingly, the waters just off the mansion's shores were the site of a multiple drowning in July 1895, when a small schooner carrying a Catholic priest, his sister, and her family went down in a summer squall. Some area residents claimed their ghosts can still be seen in the mansion's cupola on stormy nights. The mansion is now open to the public.

But let's get back to monsters. Chicago newspapers went wild with the story of Fay's encounter, and thousands of monster enthusiasts traveled to Lake Geneva and packed the resort town's beaches and landings in hopes of getting a peek at the creature dubbed Jenny (or Genny).

Things eventually quieted down. Then ten years later, in 1902, Mrs. D. Reid and five other people camping in the lake's Reid Park reported that they saw a creature "coiling and rolling about in the water not far from shore," according to a September 28 article in the *Milwaukee Sentinel*. The article was subtitled, "Length of the Amphibious Reptile Estimated from 25 to 65 feet." It went on to say:

> A sea serpent actually appeared in Geneva Lake Wednesday afternoon. There is no disputing the fact, for his snakeship came to the surface of the water in broad daylight. . . . It was no ordinary water snake, either, but a serpent somewhere from twenty-five to eighty feet long. The reptile would not lie still to be

measured, and in his convolutions and evolutions it was difficult to give any satisfactory estimate of the actual distance between his head and tail.

The first of the party to see it was a Mrs. Buckingham of Sharon, Wisconsin, whose son John was the captain of a Geneva Lake steamship. Mrs. Buckingham alerted Mrs. Reid and the rest of the party. Mrs. Reid's son, Willie, and a young man named Carl Henders fearlessly rowed out on the lake to see what the creature might be, but "his snakeship" immediately submerged. The group compared its length to that of the SS *Aurora*, which measured sixty-five feet in length.

The creature rose again later that year to scare the devil out of the respected Delavan preacher, Rev. M. N. Clark. But since that time, the popular lake has become such a buzzing cacophony of speedboats, personal water vehicles, water-skiers, and tour boats of every size that it must resemble nothing more than a sea of churning propellers when viewed from the lake bottom. Needless to say, Jenny, like hootenanny trio Peter, Paul, and Mary's "Puff the Magic Dragon," comes no more.

Great Lakes Lurkers

The same Native American water beings—the water spirit or panther and the great eel-like serpent—that swam around the smaller lakes of the state's interior also found their way into the Great Lakes that surround Wisconsin. Perhaps they began there.

The great eel-snake, Mishebenegeg, had a darker side, according to an article by Herbert Wagner in *Wisconsin Outdoor Journal*. Wagner says old legends hold that the eerie monster could be summoned by powerful sorcerers in order to increase their own abilities. He also said that shamans told young tribal members seeking visions as part of their spiritual development to refuse any good things offered by Mishebenegeg should they encounter one of the great snakes in their dreams.

Wagner recounted an eyewitness report of the lake serpent's magical nature told by J. G. Kohl, a German who toured Lake Superior in the mid-nineteenth century. Kohl claimed that he was present when a Native American shaman performed rituals to bring Mishebenegeg forth, and that he saw the creature rise from the lake and offer to trade the shaman lifelong health and prosperity in return for one of the shaman's children. I assume things probably went badly from there.

For sightings of Lake Michigan serpents, 1867 was a banner year—so much so that the proprietor of a Milwaukee saloon put a bounty of $1,000 on the head and body of one of the creatures, figuring he would make the money back by putting the great volume of fried lake serpent on his menu.

Racine, which lies along Lake Michigan north of the Illinois border, had its share of sightings, too. Chad Lewis includes two such reports in *Hidden Headlines of Wisconsin*. Both articles were reprinted from the *Racine Journal*.

The first one, from an article dated December 27, 1900, occurred at North Point as several workers at the Reichert Construction Company were fetching wagonloads of sand from the lakeshore. One of them alerted the others that he had seen a "fish" that measured as long as his wagon and his team of horses put together—about thirty feet—and that the water creature was still vigorously roiling the waters near the shore. By the time the others could grab their pickaxes and drive back to the sighting area, there was nothing to be seen but calm water. The same article noted that tugboats had chased a similar creature off Racine's shores two or three years earlier.

The newspaper published another big-fish story in 1909, this time theorizing that the "monster fish" was a giant sturgeon. However, at a measly four to six feet in length, this fish was no match for the North Point monster. While some species of sturgeon can reach twenty feet in length, those native to Wisconsin max out at a little over six feet.

Something Fishy in Milwaukee

Milwaukee is the state's largest city, but its outdoor features also offer ample room for lake monsters. With natural bays on Lake Michigan and three rivers, Milwaukee has a variety of freshwater surroundings for the most discriminating of serpents.

No surprise, then, that newspapers reported a cavorting creature near Jones Island in the late 1890s. The flap started when a crew of commercial fishermen saw a massive head pop out of the water near the spot where they were working at their nets. After the men had a long, goggle-eyed look at it, the head sank beneath the surface without revealing any of the rest of the body.

A man sitting on the city's Michigan Street Bridge had better luck viewing the creature around a week later when he spied a long, dull-green, snake-like thing undulating just beneath the river's surface. And during that same week, a group of young boaters in the city's bay saw the creature's head again, and another witness said he had seen the creature where the Milwaukee River emptied into the harbor. The shy beast must have decided to keep swimming, as that was the end of that lake monster flap. Perhaps it went back to Chicago, the location of many earlier sightings.

Rock River Monster

Thanks to the Great Depression–era Federal Writers Project and its Wisconsin offshoot that tracked and recorded Wisconsin folklore, this state has a good record of some unusual creatures that members of our indigenous population described in 1930s interviews with state writers. One tale called one of the more frightening beasts in this collection "The Terror of the Rock."

The story came from the Winnebago, now known as Ho Chunk, who along with the Potawatomi people once camped on the banks of the Rock River in south central Wisconsin. At that time, they said, canoers had to take care to avoid a huge water demon with a long tail, horns, sharp claws, and a massive jaw, all set on a giant, snake-like body. (The creature sounds to me like a combination of the water panther and the eel-like great serpents told of in other stories from around the state.)

This monster craved the flesh of both animals and humans, and it could yank a thirsty deer off the riverbank and swallow it in one gulp. It was crafty enough to grab humans at their most-used crossing places or flip their canoes to toss the riders down its lengthy gullet. People knew the monster was present when the water frothed and churned, and some believed there was more than one of these creatures. According to the legend, the monster migrated from the Rock to the Mississippi River with the coming of the white man, and swims there still.

Koshkonong Kreature

Another tale handed down from the Federal Writers Project came from the Potawatomi, who once camped at Lake Koshkonong near Edgerton in Rock County. The Rock River flows through this lake, and we know from the many ancient effigy mounds found around its shores that Koshkonong was a longtime center of indigenous ritual and habitation.

Those people believed that Koshkonong harbored within its 10,000 square acres a great water monster very like the one in the Rock River. This animal was highly energetic and effective at catching native people (though never white men) that tried to cross the lake at any point. Understandably, those who camped on Koshkonong's shores were very reluctant to travel on its waters, although the lake was a rich source of their staple food: wild rice.

Two young men once decided to test the monster by circling the lake in their canoes and trying to paddle faster than the creature could swim. The result was tragic. Eventually, their drowned bodies were recovered with white clay packed into their noses and ears as a sign and warning from the lake monster that it was responsible for their deaths.

The lake was also the site of a massacre of the Sauk people who were trapped on the lake's Blackhawk Island by their enemies. Their spirits are said to remain and add to the spooky ambience of the place.

Yet a third monster may lurk near Koshkonong. My book *Hunting the American Werewolf* includes a story of an incident that happened in the summer of 1972 near Highwood Street off the lake's southeast corner. Six teenagers had gone out one night to explore the apparently abandoned cottage of a woman known as a witch. They found among old collectibles and piles of magazines from the 1930s an antique iron bed frame and what looked like a book of spells. They decided to take both items with them.

The six skedaddled when an old Victrola began to tinkle a tune on its own, but a greater scare awaited them outside the cottage. They saw a dark shape begin to take form in the shadows. To their horror, it developed into a huge, upright wolf that lunged at them. The teens shrieked and ran. They later reported that they felt a strong sense of evil around the entity, although that may have been partly because of guilt over their trespassing and theft.

The area where this occurred was not only once the site of a Native American village but also of a group of animal effigy mounds. Some Native American people I've interviewed have suggested that such areas are still guarded by spirit entities invoked long ago by shamans. Perhaps that explains the materializing werewolf, or perhaps not. But throw in a twentieth-century witch, the lake monster, drifting spirits from a long-ago massacre, and together they make Lake Koshkonong look like a center of high strangeness, indeed.

Lake Monster Roundup: Sightings Statewide

Resort-riddled Pewaukee Lake was a hub for southern Wisconsin vacationers in the 1890s, but may also have been a hub for lake monsters, according to an article by Maura DeMet in the *Milwaukee Journal* of November 1, 1984. Titled "Sea Serpents Rise in Our Imaginings," it noted a "flurry of reports" in the last decade of the nineteenth century from people claiming to see unknown water beasts. One witness described the aquatic beast as a "green thing traveling like a gray streak." The story quoted State Historical Society director Charles Brown as saying another witness claimed he threw a spear at the creature but the missile simply bounced off the beast's tough hide. The lake monster swam away undisturbed. Most of the article, in fact, featured quotes from a pamphlet Brown had issued on the topic, including a few comments that implicated Oconomowoc Lake as another monster hotspot. Brown said a respected judge, Anthony Derse, testified as to the reality of that lake's "demon of the deep."

In La Crosse, which intrudes upon the Mississippi River on the western border of the state, campers claimed sightings of a horned river monster in 1901, according to the *La Crosse Daily Press* (the story again ferreted out by intrepid researcher Chad Lewis). Several men discovered a "large, snake-like" creature on a log near the river's edge, and were startled when the massive green serpent uncoiled itself and then slid smoothly into the water before churning up a frenzied parting spray of foam. The men compared the horns on its head to those of a calf.

La Crosse is also the home of two other creatures mentioned in this book: the lizard man, which appeared in town near the river, and the man bat, which showed up in 2006 near a gun club north of the city. I think making an appearance near a rifle range shows chutzpah on the part of that aerial creature.

Heading toward the state's center, Devil's Lake near Baraboo once shook from great battles between Thunderbirds and water panthers, according to *Wisconsin Indian Place Legends*. The Thunderbirds dropped their huge eggs at the water monsters, and the panthers fought back by roiling the waters back at them. The great force of the fighting carved the bluffs around the lake to make the landscape look as it does today. The Thunderbirds won and flew away to parts of the heavens unknown, but the surviving water spirits stayed behind and remain there still.

Perhaps in memoriam to these epic battles, the shores of Devil's Lake in Devil's Lake State Park are graced with ancient effigy mounds in the shapes of a great bird, a water spirit or panther, and several others. For those wondering where the devil of Devil's Lake enters into these legends, Native Americans say it doesn't. The original Ho-Chunk designation—Tamahcunchukdah—meant "Sacred Lake." As often happens with Indian place names, it was mistranslated by white settlers as Devil's Lake.

There was one more great water creature cited by indigenous people as crucial to the making of Wisconsin's topography. It was a giant snake that decided to take a little trip from its home in the northern pines to see the Mississippi River, and it must surely have been the biggest water monster of all. As the massive serpent undulated through the state's topsoil, the weight of its immense body dug out the bedrock to carve the twists and turns of the Wisconsin River. At the present Wisconsin Dells, he had to slam and bore his way through solid rock and so carved out the fantastic columns, bluffs, and canyons that now draw boatloads of tourists.

Monstrous or Mundane?

As impressive as the many eyewitness testimonies and ancient legends of water monsters in Wisconsin may be, skeptics believe some lake creatures can be explained by a variety of natural phenomena and also by known animals.

The most often mentioned culprit in the latter category is the primitive-looking sturgeon, already noted previously. With their tough scales called "scutes" and snouts shaped like chisels, they do not resemble most other fish found in the state, and as noted, can grow to around six feet in length—or much more in other parts of the world.

The alligator gar, so named because of its beak filled with gator-like teeth, is another fish that looks bizarre to those unfamiliar with it and can also grow to ten or twelve feet in length. Like the sturgeon, it has survived in its present form since prehistoric times and possesses large, armor-like scales. It can breathe above water for two hours and its unique ball-and-socket vertebrae allow it to thrash its body in the undulating fashion ascribed to most lake monsters. A large specimen wriggling through the water would be an impressive spectacle.

The only problem is that while it is distributed over the southeastern states, the alligator gar is not supposed to be found in Wisconsin. Given Wisconsin's river system, though, it isn't hard to imagine that a few individual gar fish could have wandered in over the years, or that their distribution may once have been more widespread before some waterways became fished out. Wisconsin waters do attract a smaller version of this fish, the shortnose or spotted gar.

Eels are another oft-suggested possibility as lake monster lookalikes; a forty-three-inch specimen was taken in St. Clair Lake, Michigan, as recently as 1990. But a fish that measures under four feet long would hardly be seen as a lake monster. Larger eels such as the conger may grow to twelve feet, and one of that size attacked a Scottish diver in 2004, but conger eels are sea creatures and very unlikely to live in Badger State lakes.

Sometimes very out-of-place fish do show up in Wisconsin waters. In 1908, the *Eau Claire Leader* reported that city resident James J. Raymond brought a recent catch from the Eau Claire River Dam to show off to the editor. The three-foot-long fish was a saltwater swordfish, complete with a six-inch sword! No one had a clue as to how the swordfish, still clinging to life even in the newspaper office, came to be in Eau Claire, an inland town not close even to the Great Lakes, much less the ocean. And if it is possible for one sea creature to make it here, other, more monstrous things could theoretically do so as well.

Giant old snapping turtles, otters, and beavers amplified mentally by panicked boaters have also been suggested as candidates for misidentification as lake monsters. But even unlikelier suspects have proved the basis of sightings. In 1911, several people in Delavan reported that a huge lake monster was swimming across a small downtown-area lake now called Comus. The "beast" that excited a cemetery sexton and several women turned out to be an escaped horse dripping with seaweed, bobbing as it swam.

Sometimes, the lake monsters turn out to be manufactured, literally. Two good examples can be found in the neighboring state of Michigan, according to Great Lakes chronicler Frederick Stonehouse in his book, *Haunted Lakes*. In 1908, said

Stonehouse, the resort area of Grand Traverse Bay was in the throes of monster mania, but the uproar was caused by a fake photo commissioned by a local reporter. The writer finally 'fessed up thirty years later.

Residents of the port city of Ludington, on Michigan's western shore, solved their own 1930s monster flap with the discovery of a huge, wooden, multi-sectioned serpent that was either abandoned or washed up on the beach. It measured thirty feet in length and the sight of it probably caused extreme distress to swimmers whenever its unknown operator dragged it through Lake Michigan. Its inventor had wired the contraption in such a way that its segments moved realistically, said Stonehouse. And it would not do to suggest that a few Wisconsin resort owners might not have been equally clever.

Fans of the "real, physical animal" line of thought regarding lake monsters have proposed that isolated, surviving specimens of species believed totally extinct—such as long-necked aquatic reptiles like plesiosaurs or mosasaurs—may explain Wisconsin sightings. These huge animals lived so long ago, however (the Mesozoic era, or 250 million to 67 million years), and would have required such rich and expansive habitats to support breeding populations that this scenario seems a stretch.

If it is true that most inland lakes are too small to support populations of large marine animals, the original perception by our native people that water monsters are spirit entities may also deserve our consideration. The idea is not unique in the world. For instance, the famous water monster of Loch Ness in Scotland was once rebuked by a man of God, St. Columba, as if it were a spirit subject to a higher authority. Occultist Aleister Crowley, who lived on Loch Ness from 1899 to 1913, allegedly took the opposite tack and tried to "raise" a water monster some three decades before the heyday of modern Nessie sightings. But this line of inquiry can get even murkier than the waters of Rock Lake.

It might be best to simply hope that Wisconsin's mysterious lake monsters have quietly slipped away to calmer, deeper waters, perhaps to Canada where they can amuse themselves by spooking tourist fishermen and ice hockey players.

Werewolves, Dogmen, and Other Unknown Upright Canids

The Great Spirit Wolf: Granddaddy of Unknown Canines?

In the peninsula named after the treacherous Great Lakes passage known as Death's Door, there once lived a monstrous and ferocious spirit wolf the indigenous people called Ah-ne-pe. So great was this wolf that, according to Robert E. Gard in *This is Wisconsin*, it is memorialized to this day by its namesake village in Kewanee County, Ahnepee.

This giant wolf made its reputation by raiding villages and eating the children and young women. No men, no matter how brave or skilled, could kill it. It attacked in the manner of a "rushing wind" or a "spirit in the darkness," said Gard, and its predations soon drove all the people, and even the bears and deer, from the land it inhabited. The people were afraid to so much as light a cook fire at night lest its light should give them away. Because of Ah-ne-pe, man and beast alike huddled in misery.

As often happens in tales of legendary beasts, a hero mighty enough to challenge Ah-ne-pe finally came along. He was a Potawatomi hunter known as Sha-hoka and was so fierce that he had killed many black bears, some with his bare hands. On a journey to the north, he fell in love with an Ojibwe woman, the daughter of a chieftain. But the chief would not give his daughter to Sha-hoka unless he killed the great, gray spirit wolf.

Ah-ne-pe's fame as a man-killer was such that even the great hunter Sha-hoka hesitated, cowering in his tent for days until one day his beloved stole away from her father and begged Sha-hoka to get the deed done. That revved the young man's motor back up and he began to prepare for the fight of his life. He made himself a huge, ash wood bow equipped with equally oversized arrows. Then, knowing the wolf he must fight was also part spirit, he took care to fortify his own spirit with a special preparation made for him by the top medicine man in the land. His confidence renewed, Sha-hoka set forth on the monster's trail.

He knew when he had reached the great wolf's territory, because the land lay in eerie stillness; no birds, insects, or squirrels broke the silence of the forest. At night he heard wails "like the voice of a demon seeking for evil spirits, like nothing else Sha-hoka had ever heard," said Gard. Ordinary men might have been frightened, but Sha-hoka knew it was the wolf's way of saying it knew it had finally met its match and that it wanted Sha-hoka to go away.

Sha-hoka kept up his determined quest, and one day he surprised the massive gray wolf as it hid watching him from under a pile of leaves. The chase was on. Sha-hoka taunted the wolf until it finally turned on him, bristling in fury with its red eyes flashing. Sha-hoka stood his ground and killed the animal with a deadly combination of his ax and bare hands in a struggle that went on for hours. When at last the grisly fight was over, he brought the Ojibwe chieftain Ah-na-pe's great head, and in return was given the chief's daughter at last. The couple set off to live by themselves and they made their home in the same den that had sheltered the spirit wolf, because Sha-hoka had earned the right.

The story as told by Gard does not say whether there were other wolves like Ah-na-pe, or whether the creature's spirit lived on after its earthly form died. But the tale does indicate that even in prehistoric days, some type of extraordinary wolf-like creature was known to our indigenous people. This is interesting because Wisconsin has become famous around the world as a place where people still see large, wolf-like creatures—often walking and running upright—on roadsides and even in cities. Could it be that the spirit of Ah-na-pe still roams, still wanting to devour human flesh but prevented from doing so because Sha-hoka conquered him so long ago?

As the reader will discover, this may be as good an explanation as any for the frightening canine creatures reported by many dozens of modern-day Wisconsinites.

The Beast of Bray Road

The revelation that large, upright wolf-like creatures apparently roam the state was first brought to light in a December 31, 1991, story in the former Walworth County newspaper, *The Week*, a publication that was based in Delavan and served the entire county and beyond. (It ceased operation in 2009.)

The reporter who wrote that story happened to be this author. I had received a tip from a local freelancer that people around my hometown of Elkhorn were saying they had seen some kind of fur-covered creature with the head of a wolf or German shepherd. What frightened many was that they observed the creature walking or running on its hind legs, kneeling, or using its paws to hold things. These actions made them think the creature was not your average dog, wolf, or coyote. For lack of a better word, they were calling it a werewolf.

My editor thought I should investigate the allegations, and I set off with tape recorder in hand and tongue planted firmly in cheek. I found, to my surprise, that the county's animal control officer, Jon Fredrickson, knew all about these rumors, because people had been calling him to ask about the "thing" they had seen. He showed me the manila file folder in which he had been stashing these reports; it was labeled "Werewolf." Now, even if Fredrickson had meant that word in a slightly sarcastic way, the fact that a county official had an active file folder marked "Werewolf" was news. My own hunt was on.

The folder's contents gave me a list of potential eyewitnesses to interview. And as I met with each person, it seemed to me that not one of them was crazy, likely to have been impaired by drugs or alcohol, or had anything to gain by making it up. Most of the sightings had occurred on or in the vicinity of a two-mile stretch of pavement just east of Elkhorn called Bray Road, and the time frame of the sightings ranged from several years to several months earlier.

I interviewed Lori Endrizzi, a single mom who had encountered the creature in 1989 as it knelt by the side of the road holding some dead animal in its upturned paws. She said that if there was such a thing as a werewolf, it would look like this creature.

Another witness was teenager Doris Gipson, who had seen it on Bray Road on the evening of Halloween that year. She felt her car bump something, and fearing she had hit a dog, she stopped and got out of the car. When she saw the six-foot, fur-covered canine she described as no mere dog, she immediately got back into the car and was terrified to see that it was running hard after her on two legs, its chest heaving, claws extended. It lunged for her blue Plymouth Sundance and left scratch marks on the rear bumper that I later saw and photographed. She felt lucky to have escaped.

There were a surprising number of others. A small group of junior high students were out sledding on nearby Bowers Road when they saw a "dog" stand up and then chase them on its hind legs. A longtime area farmer spied a huge, unknown canine by his rock pile, and several other farmers discovered giant, dog-like prints in their fields. One farmer's wife met the creature in a cornfield as she drove through it to bring a hot lunch to her husband.

I was convinced that these people were indeed seeing something, although I strongly doubted it was an actual werewolf. I finally titled my finished article "The Beast of Bray Road," because "beast" is a far more generic and inclusive term than werewolf, and we printed it. The story went national within weeks, and more witness reports from other parts of Wisconsin and even other states began making their way to me. The TV show *Inside Edition* came to Elkhorn and filmed a segment about the beast, and so did every other southern Wisconsin TV and radio news show. The legend of The Beast of Bray Road had been officially born.

Little did I know that not only had I witnessed the legend's birth, but I would watch it grow to maturity as sightings and reports continued to pour in from around the world.

The Overbearing Bearwolf

Most descriptions of the creature I prefer to call by the less Hollywood-ized term "manwolf" have remained remarkably consistent over time and across the U.S. Over and over again I hear the descriptions "head like a wolf or German shepherd," "standing between five and seven feet tall," and "covered in dark, shaggy fur," which may range from very dark brown to gray or black. The minor variations are the same that one might expect to see between individuals of any natural wolf pack. But there may be a subspecies of the unknown, upright canine that can throw a little more weight around.

Near Wausau in Marathon County, area hunters have whispered since the late 1970s and early '80s about seeing a bulky, wolf-headed creature they dubbed the "bearwolf." Researcher Todd Roll remembers hearing about it during his years in high school at that time. A street that leads north out of the city toward the area where the broad-chested canines were said to lurk became known as Bearwolf Road instead of its official name, Burek Avenue.

According to Roll, those who had seen the bearwolf said it was larger than any dog species, had black fur, and had a face more like a dog or wolf than a bear. At least one observer saw it walk upright.

In 2004, a student at a school near Wausau where Roll was lecturing told him that the student's two teen siblings had seen an animal the size of a deer that appeared to be half wolf and half bear, with yellow eyes and a tail like that of a wolf and a thick, dark mane of bushy hair on its neck.

That same year, a woman named Summer Theobald e-mailed me that she had seen a similar animal in Oconto County near the Michikauee Flowage, not far from Lake Michigan. Her sighting had occurred in 1998 as she and an aunt were driving near the flowage area and something rustling in the grass near the road caught her eye. The "something" then stood up on it hind legs and Theobald realized she was looking at what appeared to be a dark-furred dog about seven feet tall, except that its body seemed bulkier than a canine form should be. She and her aunt kept driving, and the creature ran off in the opposite direction.

Sightings of this thick-chested creature with a canine head seem to occur in an arc that extends from Wausau to Green Bay and then a bit farther south into Washington County. That is where a man would have an encounter in autumn 2006, with what sounded like exactly the same animal, and the whole world would hear about it.

Holy Hill's Unholy Terror

On the night of November 9, 2006, Steven Krueger was driving the highways and byways of Washington County at his preferred time of operation, about 1:30 A.M. This was when the fewest drivers were on the road, which made his frequent stops to pick up road-killed deer much safer to negotiate.

Krueger had contracted with the state's Department of Natural Resources to remove roadside animal carcasses. They would give him a list of reported kills, and the thirty-nine-year-old, six-foot-tall Krueger would methodically cruise the darkened countryside to find and tag the dead deer and then hoist them into the back of his truck. He carried a set of aluminum ATV ramps to help lift the heavier animals.

The small deer carcass he spied crumpled on the shoulder of State Highway 167 was not on his list, but he stopped anyway. The deer was light and limp enough that he was able to sling it atop the pile of already collected carcasses with little trouble, and it landed partly on the ramps in the truck bed. Since this deer was not already accounted for in his paperwork, Krueger left the light on over the truck bed and got into his cab to fill out a tag. The amber light on top of the cab flashed as well, making the truck a beacon of light on the dark road.

Given the eeriness of that particular site, Krueger was probably glad to have the place well-illuminated. His truck was parked just east of the entrance to Holy Hill, a spectacular Roman Catholic shrine with lighted twin spires soaring over the rolling, wooded hills around it. The streets near the shrine are filled with secluded subdivisions and bear colorful names such as Troll Hill Road.

Krueger was startled when a sharp shake to his truck interrupted his paperwork. He thought at first that it might be wind, but the truck shook again even harder, and there was no wind. He looked at the big side mirror outside his cab window and saw something unbelievable reflected there. Behind the truck bed stood a wolf-like creature over six feet tall, with pointed ears and a long muzzle. It was extending one big paw into the truck as if reaching for the deer Krueger had just thrown in. But there was something different about this animal as Krueger, an avid hunter and outdoorsman, noticed.

While the head was that of a wolf, he said, its torso appeared thicker and broader than a canine's. When he realized that he could not identify it as a bear or a wolf or anything else that he knew of, he became deeply frightened and sped off. As he stepped on the gas, he heard first the thud of the fresh carcass hitting the pavement and then a sharper noise that he recognized as one of his ATV ramps. The knowledge that the unknown, furry creature must have pulled them out with its paws made him feel an even deeper sense of panic.

After pausing at an intersection a few miles away, he decided to go back to retrieve the ramp. He approached the area very cautiously, but could see no sign of the ramp, deer, or creature. None of them were ever found, although many people combed the adjacent area. Krueger also reported the incident to the Washington County Sheriff's Department that night. From there the encounter made its way to local newspapers and TV shows, all of whom mistakenly called the creature a "Bigfoot." Krueger said that he never used that word, and that what he saw was no Bigfoot, but the word lit a firestorm of publicity.

It makes Krueger's case even stronger when it's noted that he was not the only witness to see a bearish, wolfish creature in the Washington County area.

Painting contractor Rick Selcherk, who was also thirty-nine at the time of his sighting, was headed to work at dawn in November 2004, when he saw a shaggy, dark-brown creature the size of a deer, but with pointed ears and a doglike muzzle, cross Slinger Road just south of State Highway 60. He estimated it weighed up to two hundred pounds and said it looked like a combination of a bear and some other creature.

In November 2006, just three days after Steve Krueger's sighting, two men saw another deer-sized, unidentifiable creature cross Shalom Drive near West Bend on all fours. Its head was like a wolf's, they said, but its furry muscular body was too big to be a wolf, yet too lean to be a bear.

About that same time, two young boys in the town of Merton told their parents they saw a large, hairy monster in the woods near the yard where they were playing, according to Milwaukee TV station WISN. Another person reported via e-mail that he and an employee had seen not one but two furry, upright creatures around 1997, just a quarter mile north of Holy Hill. And in June 2007, Krueger had a second glimpse of a huge canine that stood four feet tall at the shoulders on all fours, watching him from under a mailbox that Krueger later measured. It was located on the same DNR contract route as the first creature incident. Krueger quit the deer collection business soon after that and is now a syndicated cartoonist with a comic called *Moose Lake* that caters to fishermen and other outdoor enthusiasts. The bearwolf is noticeably absent from his work.

As for the true nature of the bearwolf, there are sever possible natural explanations: a bear with mange (although no one has reported seeing bald spots), a subspecies of wolf with a larger body, or a wolf-dog hybrid. None of these break any new ground.

Nor is the idea of bear-canine combos completely novel. In London, England, in 1878, numerous witnesses reported seeing a creature that looked like a bear crossed with a dog.

There is also the supernatural, guardian spirit theory, which comes to mind when one considers Holy Hill's sacred status and the fact that the hill itself was considered sacred both by the settlers and the Native Americans who lived there earlier.

Then there is the fact that this same area is the site of the Civil War–era Goat Man tale and was also haunted by a strange hermit. It just gets spookier and spookier.

Steve Krueger, however, is convinced that what he saw was a flesh-and-blood animal—it would have taken one very strong spirit entity to have pulled that deer off his truck. And even though several years have passed, Krueger would still like his ATV ramp back.

Multiple Manwolves

Since sightings of upright, wolf-like creatures date back at least to 1936 and range not only across Wisconsin but most of the United States, if these are flesh-and-blood animals, then a breeding population must exist. The fact is that witnesses have indeed reported seeing more than one creature at a time in Wisconsin and other states. One such witness who passed a stringent polygraph test administered by an expert hired by the History Channel is Katie Zahn of Janesville.

Katie was only fifteen in the summer of 2003 when she and three friends took a drive to the 168-acre nature preserve called Avon Bottoms in southwestern Rock County. Part of their mission that day was to look for a haunted bridge local teenlore said existed somewhere in the scenic, marshy area.

There was also an urban legend about a scientist killed by a breeding experiment gone wrong somewhere in the preserve, Katie noted. Her two male friends had also brought BB guns, and they stopped in a field to do a little practice shooting as Katie and her female friend waited by a graveled area near the car. The young women were both a little disturbed to see a giant paw print with claw marks in a muddy patch next to the gravel. It proved to be a bad omen of what was to come.

It wasn't long before the two young men came running as if for their lives, yelling terrified warnings at the girls to also run and get back in the car. To Katie's amazement, the boys were being chased by what looked like a huge dog or wolf running on its hind legs. Katie said the creature's gait was "kind of wobbly," but it stood six to seven feet tall and was covered with fur. The four teens dove into the safety of their vehicle and drove off while the creature, as is usual in these cases, loped away in another direction.

Once they had caught their breath, the teens decided to look for the haunted bridge despite the frightening encounter, since they knew it was not near the field, and soon found it. Feeling they had put a safe distance between themselves and the shaggy beast, they got out of the car and peered over the side of the bridge at the creek.

There, Katie said, they saw three of the same type of creature that had chased the boys. These animals seemed a little smaller than the other one, she said, and they were bent over the stream and drinking out of their "hands," rather than lapping the water like a dog. As soon as they noticed the teens, the creatures stood up on their hind legs and then began to wade, upright, across the stream toward Katie and her friends. The four again quickly decided to get in the car and leave the park for good this time, but not before Katie had a very careful look at the three creatures. I quoted her in *Hunting the American Werewolf*:

Their faces were thin, with a long nose, pointy ears that went straight up. They had thinner necks, like a human. They were walking straighter than the first one. They had broad shoulders, tails, and their legs were bigger on top and smaller at the ankle but they had really big feet, which were longer than a dog paw, like oval. We were fifteen to twenty feet away.

They had long claws on more humanlike hands, and their teeth were like a dog's teeth but real long. They were like half-human, half-dog. Their hips were like a human's with longer legs than a dog would be. They were like human, but covered with fur and with a dog head. The first one we saw had seemed a lot more angry.

Their fur was long, it hung from the body straight and was thin enough to move with the breeze, like ours. I am positive they were not people in animal suits.

We all got really warm. I don't know if it was adrenalin but we were all sweating instantly. They got just across the stream and then stopped, and that was when we got back in the car. I don't think they wanted to hurt us, they just wanted us to leave. They didn't act mean or anything. We didn't look in their eyes, though as soon as they looked at us, we ran.

Katie's friends decided they did not want to talk about the story—ever—but Katie told her father all about it as soon as she got home. They both kept it to themselves after that. Two years later her father attended one of my book signings and told me about Katie's encounter, and I asked to interview her.

I was more impressed by Katie than I had expected to be. Teenagers tend to be disrespected in general, and I was sure people would find her story suspect both because of her age and because of the story's amazing details. The fact, however, that she told only her father and then kept quiet about what she had witnessed told me that Katie was not using the story to seek attention. Moreover, she passed the TV show *Monsterquest*'s polygraph exam with a conclusion that showed absolutely no indication of deception, and she has never wavered from the story details since.

Also, the sighting occurred in daylight at fairly close range and was witnessed by four people at the same time, which rules out individual imagination or hallucination. Her description tallied very closely with those of other witnesses around the state. The three animals' cupped paws and their behavior of drinking from them both sound somewhat unusual, but some mammals can achieve this gesture by flexing their knuckle joints to form what biologists call a "convergent paw."

Did Katie and her friends happen upon a family of manwolves, with the first, larger one chasing the boys in order to scare them away from what may have been the females and/or juveniles in its pack or family? It certainly did seem that Katie and her friends saw a pack, at least, of whatever the creatures were.

In another possible indication that there are more breeding pairs of huge, wolf-like creatures in Wisconsin, Kenosha resident Rick Renzulli says he saw two such canines crossing a road in front of him, one after the other.

In October 1984, Renzulli was up early at about 5 A.M., rounding the curve on County Highway ML, west of Kenosha, on his way to work as a concrete finisher. He was approaching a small cemetery and was only up to about fifteen miles per hour after stopping at an intersection with Green Bay Road, when something dashed from the area of the cemetery and in front of his 1978 Caravan Suburban. It was on all fours and stood as high as the Suburban's hood at the shoulders. Renzulli estimated its length at between seven and nine feet and said it was three to four times the size of a St. Bernard he used to own.

Its eyes shone back at him from the glare of his headlights, and Renzulli said it appeared angry. "I thought of evil," he said.

No sooner had that registered than a second creature followed the first. It was similar in appearance, but smaller. Both animals had bristles on the backs of their necks and shoulders and long legs that would rule out something like feral hogs.

Although they ran on all fours rather than upright, Renzulli still had the impression that the creatures he saw were not natural. And the fact that they appeared in the immediate vicinity of an old cemetery lends a supernatural overtone to the story. Some might think that rather than representing a breeding pair of manwolves, these were another example of spirit guardians trying to drive intruders from the graveyard. And the fact that they did not run upright leaves the possibility that they were some kind of huge dog hybrid, either feral or escaped.

I am not sure which of all these alternatives I'd prefer.

The Milwaukee Manwolf

Over the past eighteen years I have received many dozens of reports of large, upright canines in Wisconsin and the world—enough to fill three separate books that have been published on the topic. But one continues to stand out in my mind, partly because of the harrowing nature of the encounter and partly because I found unexplainable and clear footprints in a mudhole nearby.

On Saturday, June 30, 2007, a call came about a sighting only a few days earlier on June 26. The three young adult witnesses swore they had not been drinking or doing drugs previous to the sighting.

The site, Fitzsimmons Road, runs east-west between South Milwaukee and Racine and is partly closed off by a barrier just after a few residential blocks, because at the end of its one-mile length, it crumbles into an eroded cliff over Lake Michigan. This has given the road a longtime reputation as a haunted lover's lane. The witnesses had set off on foot about 1 A.M. the night of June 26, their way lit by a three-quarter moon and a streetlight.

The group consisted of Jonathan Hart, then twenty-five; Jonathan's brother Benjamin Hart, then eighteen; plus a twenty-two-year-old friend of Jon's who I will call Jane and two eighteen-year old friends of Ben's, Breonna and Shawna (last names withheld). As they proceeded down the dark lane, they all heard a high-pitched, drawn-out scream coming from somewhere in the cornfield to the north of the road. (To the south was a wheatfield.) It sounded like a woman, said Jane, yet they knew it was not human.

They had walked about half the length of the road and were still next to the cornfield and about one-eighth mile from a small wooded area that leads to the cliff, when Ben spotted a pair of almond, yellowish eyes glaring at them from the brush. Breonna and Shawna then returned to the car.

Jane, Ben, and Jon decided to see what the creature was. Jane's flashlight revealed a kind of furry, canid creature crouching at least forty feet away. To their amazement it rose onto its hind legs and faced them, growling.

Its shaggy fur was bi-colored: light tan in front and the rest of it dark brown. Ben, who stands more than six feet, said the creature was as tall, or taller, than he was. The creature then moved one doglike forelimb as if getting ready to come toward them, and the three humans shrieked and ran. Ben was in the lead, followed by Jane and then Jon. They could hear the animal's feet hitting the ground with the weight and rhythm of a biped, but faster than a human's feet would go, they said. It closed the distance between them in seconds, and they felt it could easily have caught them had it wanted to.

At one point, the creature did catch up to Jon, close enough that he could feel its body heat and that he "felt its presence," as he put it. The creature grazed the back of his shirt with the tips of its claws, leaving two sets of triple five-eighths-inch slashes about one inch apart on the back of his shirt. Jon said that he felt warm at the point where his shirt was touched, but the rest of his body felt cold.

Just before they reached the barrier and streetlight, the sound of the footsteps stopped. The creature was gone. But it would not be forgotten. As they ran, Jane said, she had turned several times to focus her flashlight on Jon and the creature to make sure Jon was still there and could glimpse the dark form behind him.

Jon and Ben's mother told me later that her eighteen-year-old sobbed as he related the story and that he was truly frightened, but it was their aunt who contacted me.

The witnesses said this was not a bear, human in a suit, or Bigfoot, based on what they saw and how it moved—on its toes like a dog. Jon, who was closest, said that it also smelled bad.

I arrived to investigate a few days later and walked the road with Ben, Jon, their mother, aunt, and Jane in bright daylight. We found some canine prints on the sand point at the end of the road that measured about three inches long and could have belonged to a large dog, but not to a wolf-like creature that stood six feet tall.

As we walked back down the road we took searched some paths and tractor lanes that led beyond the road. Off a deer trail into the woods on the north side of the road was a clay-mud water hole covered with animal tracks. There were prints from what looked like some larger type of canid mixed with numerous deer tracks and a few others identical to the three-inch prints we found earlier at the end of the road. The larger prints measured about eight inches long and showed claw marks.

It looked like some predator had ambushed a deer; the deer's prints angled deeply into the edge of the clay. Sometimes footprints left in mud will spread and widen as the mud settles out, creating falsely large tracks. In this case, the other animal's three-inch prints were identical in size to the others found in the cliff sand, and the deer prints also measured a normal size.

Jon gave me the clawed shirt. The two sets of tears were very clean, with no detectable residue of any kind. It did seem to me that an animal lunging forward might have exerted enough force to have completely shredded the shirt down to the bottom, but Jon said he never felt the claws on his skin.

The fact that the brothers' mother and aunt vouched for the boys' account of the events and also accompanied them when we examined the site did give me more confidence in their report. The late Janesville film maker John Gage also told me he felt they were truthful after he filmed—and grilled—them a year after the sighting for a documentary video he was working on at the time.

I conducted another phone interview with Jon Hart on April 19, 2010, and he reaffirmed all of his prior statements. "It was there," he said. "I can still picture it in my mind clear as day. It's totally inexplicable."

Badgerland Hellhounds

Most of the unknown, upright canines reported in Wisconsin do behave very strangely by walking and running upright or using their paws like hands, but their eyes reflect a normal yellow-green and they do not usually do anything that goes beyond what is possible for a natural animal.

A few sightings, however, have involved creatures that morph, materialize inside houses, and glare with eyes glowing a decidedly unnatural crimson. Some people call them hellhounds, after the ancient and widespread notion that fierce spectral canines guarded the gates of the underworld. Hellhounds have also traditionally served as psychopomps, or entities that guide the dead to their afterlives.

The mysterious beasts seen in Wisconsin, however, also seem to have a lot in common with legends of black phantom dogs of Great Britain, whose stories often date back many centuries and are found in every part of the British Isles. A few of the many colorful names for this historic creature of the British Isles, varying according to location, include the Gyrtrash, Black Shuck, Padfoot, Skriker, and Gwyllgi. (Harry Potter fans will note that author J. K. Rowling borrowed the name Padfoot from these legends to serve as a nickname for one shapeshifting wizard.)

Like the Beast of Bray Road and other wolf-like creatures of Wisconsin, phantom dogs are most often encountered in churchyards and graveyards and along roads, especially at crossroads. They are usually described as larger than a normal dog and dark in color, although in Great Britain phantom hounds may sometimes be white or gray. The *cu sith*, fairy dogs of Scotland, stand out among this scruffy lot because their fur is green!

While so far no one has reported seeing any dogs the color of summer grass in the Badger State, the small community of Caryville on the Chippewa River near Eau Claire is said to have a whole pack of black, red-eyed hellhounds that rampage down Caryville Road on stormy nights. They are supposed to live on an island across from Meridean Boat Landing, where legend says they guard the site of an old sanatorium that once stood on an island connected to the river's shore by ferry. It is doubtful the small farming and lumber community that called the island home ever had a sanatorium, but some people say the dogs can still be heard barking and howling before their midnight run.

Dogs that guard an island are also part of the lore of Okauchee Lake in Waukesha County, according to a musician named Scott who spent his childhood summers at an aunt's cottage on the western shore of the lake. The cottage was near an island with the ruins of an old mansion. Area residents believed the mansion's grounds were patrolled by red-eyed, black dogs that walked upright, but Scott never dared to go find out for himself if the legend was true. His family called the isle Haunted Island.

Okauchee Lake possesses a few other notable oddities. It has several small islands, and a vacant piece of land called Party Island is a destination for fun-loving boaters. A place on the northwest side of the lake is nicknamed Crazyman's Island. The western shore of the lake also once held an ancient, thirty-foot diameter conical burial mound as well as other sites sacred to Native Americans.

Phantom Black Dogs of Eau Claire

It is one thing to contemplate phantom dogs barking at the moon on a remote island, but quite another to encounter a possible hellhound in your own home or yard. This frightening scenario happened to two unrelated Eau Claire residents as they went about their daily lives.

One, a young man who was renting a room from a friend on Cameron Street in May 2003, reported that he woke up one day at 2:30 P.M., while it was very light out, and walked from his room to the bathroom. His business there successfully concluded, he started to return to his room but was stopped by a six-and-a-half-foot-tall, black creature with a wolf-like head and a human body standing just outside the bathroom door.

The creature appeared very muscular, and the man estimated it would have weighed three hundred pounds had it been a human. It had glistening, oily skin and huge claws, and its snarl revealed sharp fangs. Its eyes were not red but yellow, and the man thought that it meant to kill him, even though its form seemed a bit transparent. The man insisted he was fully awake at this point.

He was awake enough, at least, to reach for a nearby baseball bat with which to defend himself, but the creature turned its head as if startled by something else and then vanished. The man tried to write the incident off as some kind of fluke hallucination, but since it happened in broad daylight while he was wide awake, he would never be convinced that it was all in his head. And the fact that someone else in his town had a very similar experience helps bolster his strange story.

Another man wrote to say he had seen almost the same thing in his Eau Claire yard at dusk in the summer of 2008. The creature was dark brown rather than black and had a bit shorter muzzle, but otherwise was almost the same as a sketch I had drawn of the first man's creature. He said it moved like a "ninja" between his truck and garage; then like the Cameron Street creature, it simply melted into the air and was gone.

Unlike the first man, however, this one wasn't afraid of what he saw. In fact, he said, a not unwelcome idea that the shadowy entity might be a personal "spirit guardian" occurred to him.

Neither man ever saw his muscle-bound visitor again. Whether these canine humanoids were true hallucinations, visitors from some other dimension, remnants of some ancient earth spirit matrix attached to the Eau Claire area, or some other phenomenon of which we simply have no knowledge, remains to be seen. And that leaves us to wonder which lucky Eau Claire resident will see it next.

Madison Morpher

If true werewolves did exist, they would necessarily require the skill to "morph," short for metamorphosing, or changing from one shape to another. But just because something doglike happens to morph does not necessarily mean it is a werewolf. The tradition of beings called shapeshifters, which are generally thought to be either unknown spirit entities or the nebulous results of ritual magic, weaves through the darker lore of almost all human cultures.

Shapeshifters are not just spirit relics of the past, either. One Madison man, a graduate student in several sciences at the university, told me that he had witnessed what seemed to be a morphing creature on a sidewalk of a residential area in the Isthmus, the bridge of land between Lakes Mendota and Monona.

He was out walking in May 2004 at a late hour, he said, because he and his girlfriend had quarreled and he felt he needed to get away for a bit. As he walked, he noticed something moving in the shadows under a streetlight. At first he thought it was a person on all fours, except that it was not crawling like a human on its knees would do. The creature began to move faster until it appeared more like a canine, its limbs flying so fast that it reminded him of a very gymnastically talented break dancer. It even seemed to him at one point that there were two creatures, spinning together in a way that boggled his mind.

The man stood about twenty feet from the spectacle, he said. His first instinct had been to run but he stood transfixed as the "thing" continued its wild dance. When at last it stopped, it turned and looked at him with the deep-set eyes of a great ape—the dark hairy body had taken on the head and face of a gorilla. The man ran back to his girlfriend's house and rang the doorbell until she let him back in, his face white from shock.

I have no idea what he saw, but it surely does not sound like any sort of natural animal. It did remind me, as I noted in *Hunting the American Werewolf*, of the Egyptian god Thoth, who could appear as a baboon or dog-ape. Coincidentally, the ancient *Book of Thoth* consists partly of magic spells, some of which involve the alleged power to transform one's shape.

Or might it have been another example of phantom dogs? Ghostly mutts do not come with pedigrees; there are no breeding standards for hellhounds. Who is to say that they might not be able change their looks or even species with each appearance?

I am still hoping that some Wisconsin Scotsman will report seeing one of those emerald-green cu sith. If the other phantom dogs can cross the Atlantic and swim the Great Lakes to reach us, I don't see why the Scottish spirit animal couldn't do the same.

The Witiko

A number of writers have attempted to link Wisconsin's unknown canines with a creature common to the traditions of Algonquian-speaking indigenous nations, the Wendigo, or Witiko. I have counted around one dozen spelling variations of this name. I will use Witiko, as it seems closest to most pronunciations.

The problem with this comparison is that the majority of historical, native descriptions of this creature do not sound at all like a fur-covered upright canine. Witiko is an interesting though tragic figure in its own right. Its home is in the northern forests, where the twin specters of starvation and freezing temperatures stalk humans during the brutal winter that comes every year.

As it sometimes happened in the past, a person might be so desperate from the cold or the lack of food that he or she might be driven to eat the flesh of another person in order to survive. Once gone cannibal, the person is both shunned and feared. The cannibal has started down the path to becoming a Witiko. His heart will turn to ice, he may grow to the height of the tallest pines, and he will hunt his fellow humans for food. Strangely, he may be blinded and confused by human excrement. Luckily, that particular substance is usually readily available as soon as potential victims catch sight of the fearsome creature.

Guardian helper spirits and human ingenuity usually play the biggest part in defeating a Witiko, however. George Nelson, a Canadian trapper who kept a meticulous journal on the beliefs of the Algonquian people with whom he lived, was very interested in their stories of the Witiko. (The book, *The Orders of the Dreamed*, which includes his journal, was mentioned in the story of the Little People.) Nelson wrote of the creatures that "to add to their dread, they are represented as possessing much of the Power of Magicians . . . at every step the Earth shakes."

Nelson related a tale he had heard about a village that had banded together one winter for protection against the Witiko. Deciding to be proactive rather than waiting for it to come and eat them, the people designed a big wooden trap for the monster and camouflaged it between two great pines. All they needed was a human willing to sit in the trap to act as bait.

An elderly woman finally volunteered to sacrifice herself, seeing that she was near the end of her years anyway. She took her place up in the tree branches, and soon the Great Horror's heavy footsteps were heard thumping through the woods. It saw the old woman right away, but not the trap hidden by pine boughs, and informed her that he was about to grind her up with his giant teeth.

The woman stood her ground and told the creature that her people had abandoned her there because she was so old and they wished to be rid of her. She begged the Witiko to take her out of the tree.

The Witiko figured he would have to do that in order to eat her, so he bent forward and immediately sprang the trap upon himself. The villagers who had been hiding nearby rushed at the immobilized monster and killed it with many blows of their axes and knives. That took care of at least one Witiko. And the brave woman was able to live out her years in honor for having saved her people.

Other stories vary; one recurring theme is that when the monster is killed, either its heart of ice falls out and melts or only a shriveled version of the person the Witiko once was will remain.

Lumberjack Legends

Some people think it may be northern Wisconsin's long winters that leave people with nothing better to do than to make up imaginary animals; others insist that creatures like the Hodag and the Snallygaster are rare but actual animals that inhabit the darkest reaches of the state's vast forest preserves.

The legions of lumberjacks that swarmed Wisconsin's vast stands of timber in the latter half of the nineteenth century were especially creative at naming and describing these wild companions of Paul Bunyan and Babe the Blue Ox. Real or invented, the critters present one formidable bestiary.

Hodag: The Monster That Wasn't

Residents of Rhinelander love their hometown monster. A giant green replica of the Hodag stands proudly outside the town's visitor center, and Rhinelander holds a festival in its honor every year. It even boasts its own Wisconsin historical marker that is a bit of a spoiler for true believers.

The Hodag dates back to 1896 when its creator, a well-known prankster and lumberjack of the Rhinelander area, announced that he had discovered a great, hairy black beast hiding out in the trees around Rice Creek. Gene Shepard made his story a real whopper, describing how he piled rocks in front of the monster's den to trap it and then poking a chloroform-soaked rag inside to knock the creature out.

For proof, he offered a seven-foot wooden model carved by artist Luke Kearney. Kearney spared no detail, adding Texas steer-like horns, a back ridge of twelve pointed spikes, and long, curved claws on each foot to the sculpture. The enterprising Shepard took his Hodag on a ten-year tour of county fairs, wiring it so that given a dimly lit environment, it could be made to seem as if it moved. The exhibit tents were dark enough so that Shepard's Hodag sculpture fooled a fair share of those who coughed up the coin to see it. They were further impressed with Shepard's claims about the Hodag's diet, which consisted of a white bulldog fed to it every Sunday. The feeding was never done publicly.

In 1906, after ten years of travel and display, the old Hodag tale was losing some of its luster. Shepard thought up a brilliant ploy to renew interest in his invention. He staged a "recapture" of the Hodag, complete with a photograph of men armed with pitchforks, axes, and rifles, holding the creature at bay. In the foreground lay the beast's prone "victim." Shepard himself stood behind the sculpture of the Hodag, flourishing a hefty stick. The photo caused a sensation and the Hodag's popularity skyrocketed.

Its notoriety gradually waned again, but like any good monster, the black beast roused itself for one more round. In summer 1952, the *Rhinelander Daily News* declared that Hodag tracks had been found on the property of George DeByle and that a group of men had set out to capture the beast. The story detailed the bloody goring of citizen Don Pecor. Success was finally achieved via Shepard's original Hodag-fighting weapon, chloroform on a stick. A photo showing the victorious hunters circling the Hodag provided visual evidence for those gullible enough to believe it. The new Hodag was the work of woodcarver Ed Stoltz, who had produced a two-hundred-pound statue fashioned of white pine.

Shepard exhibited that Hodag at the Oneida County fair and eventually put it to rest at the city's Logging Museum. The modern version that greets all visitors to Rhinelander is much larger than its wooden predecessors and is painted a more tourist-friendly green. True fans can buy all manner of Hodag merchandise, from T-shirts to snow globes, in the visitor center's gift shop.

Paul Bunyan's Pets

A myriad of other legendary lumber beasts hopped, flew, and wriggled through the old pine forests, according to state folklorists Robert E. Gard and L. G. Soren. They called it "Paul Bunyan's natural history" in their book *Wisconsin Lore* and noted that their collection of unknown animal tales sprang from sources both reliable and unreliable.

Their list is alphabetical and starts with the axe-handle hound, a large dachshund-like canine that sneaks into camps at night and devours axe handles. It ends with the whirligig fish, scaled creatures that swim so fast around ice-fishing holes that they eventually twirl themselves right up onto the ice and then into waiting frying pans.

In between those two creatures lie such puzzlements as the argopelter, a white tree-dweller whose chief amusement was to throw lethal hunks of wood down on unsuspecting humans, and the gumberoo, which resembled a walking football larger than a bear. The gumberoo's tough hide resisted bullets and arrows; the lumberjack's only defense was to light it on fire and watch it explode.

Another huge and vicious creature was the rumptifusel, which looked a lot like a long mink coat. It was sneaky, too, and would hang limp on a tree until some freezing lumberjack came along and tried to wear it. At that point, the woodsman became the rumptifusel's dinner.

Even weirder was the gyascutus, which might have been taken for a deer if not for its long ears, huge fangs, long tail, and legs that telescoped inward so that the creature could balance on hillsides. It subsisted on rocks and tough lichens, said Gard and Sorden, so that at least it was no danger to men.

The same could not be said of the silver cat, a giant feline with feathery long fur at the ends of its ears, vertically slit red eyes, and a lethal tail that had a flat side for clubbing prey in the head and a spiked side to jab and pull the victim to its mouth. Lumberjacks also had to beware of the moskittos, mosquitoes so oversized that one could arch itself across a stream and then drain the crews steering log rafts as they passed downriver beneath its bloated belly.

True escape from the moskitto was difficult. If a woodsman jumped into the river to save himself, he might be taken by a cougar fish, a massive species with claws at the end of its fins, or a log gar, with teeth so like those of a saw that it could slice through bone and flesh in an instant.

Other lumber-land critters included the harmless teakettle, the sneaky hide-behind that was never seen, the poisonous hoop and snow snakes, and the backward-flying goofus bird. There were probably many others whose secrets died along with the last embers of the lumberjack campfires. Once the last stands of pine had been clear-cut and the northern lands stood denuded, there was no place left for silver cats and teakettlers to hide.

Perhaps it was their demise that made room for the Bigfoot, werewolves, and alien-like things that were to follow. At least the state has remained zoologically interesting as a result. For that, we owe them our uneasy gratitude.

Let the wild rumpus continue!

BIBLIOGRAPHY

BOOKS AND ARTICLES

Berscheid, Dewey. "Driver Yields to Visiting UFO." *Pioneer Press* (January 1973): 1, 8.

Boyer, Dennis. *Giants in the Land*. Madison, WI: Prairie Oak Press, 1997.

Brown, Jennifer S. H., and Robert Brightman. *Orders of the Dreamed*. St. Paul: Minnesota Historical Society Press, 1988.

"Catches Swordfish in Eau Claire River." *Eau Claire Leader*, Eau Claire, WI, June 18, 1908.

Coleman, Jerry D. *Strange Highways*. Alton, IL: Whitechapel Press, 2003.

Coleman, Loren, and Patrick Huyghe. *The Field Guide to Bigfoot, Yeti, and Other Mystery Primates Worldwide*. New York: Avon, 1999.

Devereaux, Paul. *Haunted Land: Investigations into Ancient Mysteries and Modern Day Phenomena*. Bath, UK: Bath, 2001.

Edmonds, Michael. "Flights of Fancy: Birds and People in the Old Northwest." *Wisconsin Magazine of History* 83: 3 (Spring 2000): 65.

Gard, Robert E. *This is Wisconsin*. Spring Green, WI: Wisconsin House, 1969.

Gard, Robert E., and Elaine Reetz. *Trail of the Serpent; Lore and Legend of the Fox River Valley*. New York: Wisconsin House, 1973.

Gard, Robert E. and L. G. Sorden. *Wisconsin Lore*. Ashland, WI: Ashland Press, 1962.

Gill, Sam D., and Irene Sullivan. *Dictionary of Native American Mythology*. New York: Oxford University Press, 1992.

Godfrey, Linda S. *Haunted Wisconsin: Ghosts and Strange Phenomena of the Badger State*. Mechanicsburg, PA: Stackpole Books, 2010.

———. *Hunting the American Werewolf*. Black Earth, WI: Prairie Oak Press, 2006.

————. *Strange Wisconsin: More Badger State Weirdness.* Madison, WI: Trails Books, 2007

Godfrey, Linda S., and Richard D. Hendricks. *Weird Wisconsin: Your Travel Guide to Wisconsin's Local Legends and Best Kept Secrets.* New York: Barnes & Noble, 2005.

Keel, John. "Even Baboons Believe in Ghosts." *FATE Magazine* 52, No. 10 (October 1999): 13.

Leary, James P. *Wisconsin Folklore.* Madison: University of Wisconsin Press, 1998.

Meldrum, Jeff. *Sasquatch: Legend Meets Science.* New York: Tom Doherty Associates, 2006.

Menn, Esther. *Wisconsin Footsteps.* WI: privately printed, 1989.

Redfern, Nick. *Memoirs of a Monster Hunter.* Franklin Lakes, NJ: New Page Books, 2007.

Sanderson, Ivan. "Wisconsin's Abominable Snowman." *Argosy* (April 1969): 27-29, 70.

Shiel, Lisa A. *Backyard Bigfoot: The True Story of Stick Signs, UFOs, and the Sasquatch.* Lake Linden, MI: Slipdown Mountains Publications, 2006.

Seubert, Greg, "Family Says Bigfoot Lives," *Marshfield News-Herald,* August 1, 1991: 3.

Stonehouse, Frederick. *Haunted Lakes: Great Lakes Ghost Stories, Superstitions, and Sea Serpents.* Duluth, MN: Lake Superior Port Cities, 1997.

"The Terror of the Rock." *Wisconsin Indian Place Legends.* Madison, WI: Folklore Section, Federal Writers' Projects, 1936.

"The Water Monster." *Wisconsin Indian Place Legends.* Madison, WI: Folklore Section, Federal Writers' Projects, 1936.

Wagner, Herbert. "Wisconsin's Monsters of the Deep." *Wisconsin Outdoor Journal* (August 1993): 68.

Woods, Lunetta. *Story in the Snow.* Lakeville, MN: Galde Press, 1997.

ONLINE SOURCES

Ames, Ann Marie. "Janesville Police Capture Monitor Lizard." *Gazette Extra,* October 6, 2010. Retrieved October 11, 2010. http://gazettextra.com/weblogs/latest-news/2010/oct/06/janesville-police-capture-monitor-lizard.

Baldwin, Chuck. "Is Bigfoot Roaming in Frankfort?" *Wausau Daily Herald,* July 28, 1992. *The W-Files.* Retrieved April 21, 2006. www.w-files.com/files/bffrankfort1991.html.

Baldwin, Chuck. "Psychic Persuades Bigfoot to Leave Farm?" *Wausau Daily Herald,* July 28, 1992. *The W-Files.* Retrieved April 21, 2006. www.w-files.com/files/bffrankfort1991.html.

Brown, Charles E. "The Serpent Bozho." Wisconsin Folklore Society, 1942. *Weird Wisconsin*. Retrieved June 7, 2004. www.weird-wi.com/lakes/brown3.html.

Brown, Dorothy Moulding. "Wisconsin Water Monsters." *Wisconsin Archaeologist Internet Archive*. Retrieved August 16, 2010. www.archive.org/stream/wisconsinarcheol17wiscrich/wisconsinar-cheol17wiscrich_djvu.txt.

Burt, Terry. "Bigfoot Was a Big Story in Cashton." *La Crosse Tribune*, July 28, 2004. Retrieved July 28, 2004. www.lacrossetribune.com/articles/2004/07/28/region/01column.txt.

"Feral Pigs." *Wisconsin Department of Natural Resources*. Retrieved September 28, 2010. http://dnr.wi.gov/org/land/wildlife/publ/wlnotebook/pig.htm.

Flynn, Courtney. "Holy Gator; Pet is No Crock." *Chicago Tribune*, July 19, 2006. Retrieved July 19, 2006.

Freeman, Richard. "Wisconsin's Missing Lake Monster Relics." *Still on the Track*. Retrieved August 16, 2010. forteanzoology.blogspot.com/2010/01/richard-freeman-wisconsins-missing-lake.html.

Galli, Toni. "UW Student Group Tries to Stop Tiger Show." *WKOW*, March 4, 2010. Retrieved September 23, 2010. http://www.wkow.com/Global/story.asp?S = 12087090&clienttype = printable.

Galli, Toni. "Wisconsin Wild Animal Show Incorporates Safety Features." *WKOW*, February 26, 2010. Retrieved Sept. 23, 2010. http://www.wkow.com/Global/story.asp?S = 12087090&clienttype = printable.

Harris, Paul. "Is This the Beast of Exmoor?" *Daily Mail*, Jan.9, 2009. Retrieved Oct. 13, 2010. http://www.dailymail.co.uk/news/article-1109174/Is-Beast-Exmoor-Body-mystery-animal-washes-beach.html.

"Is Long Lake the Home of . . . ?" *The W-Files*. Retrieved June 1, 2004. www.ufowisconsin.com/wfiles/files/lmlonglake.html.

Johnson, Johnson. "You Shot a What?" *Milwaukee Journal Sentinel*, October 1, 2007. Retrieved September 28, 2010. http://www/jsonline.com/news/29222824.html.

Johnson, Neil. "Cougar Sightings Reported, but Proof is Rare." *Janesville Gazette*, August 10, 2010. Retrieved August 13, 2010. http://gazettextra.com/new/2010/aug/13/cougar-sightings-reported-proof-rare/?print.

Kelleher, Bob. "That's No Bear—That's a Pig!" *Minnesota Public Radio*. Retrieved September 29, 2010. http://news.minnesota.publicradio.org/features/2005/10/26_kelleherb_feralpigs.

Levihn, Annie. "A Delightful Children's Book by Madisonian Jean Rennebohm Keeps Children Hopping for More," *Brava Magazine*. Retrieved September 20, 2010. http://www.bravamagazine.com/article.jsp?id = 360&department = 47

"Missing Vulture Could Pose Threat in Scottish Skies." *BBC News Glasgow & West*. Retrieved August 21, 2010. www.bbc.co.uk/news/uk -scotland-11011384?print = truee.

Nutt, Amy Ellis. "Exotic Pets; Disaster Waiting to Happen." *Star Ledger*, October 3, 2006. Retrieved September 23, 2010. http://bigcatnews .blogspot.com/2006/10/exotic-pets-disaster-waiting-to-happen.html.

"Sanctuary Took in Alligator Found in Rock County." *Channel3000.com*. Retrieved September 28, 2010. http://www.channel3000.com/print/ 24031103/detail.html.

Stephen, Jessica. "Salem Man Sentenced for Mistreating Animals," *Kenosha News*, July 9, 2010. Retrieved August 12, 2010. www.kenoshanews2.com/news/salem_man_sentenced_for _mistreating_animals_12282849.html.

"The Panther and the Terrapin." *Wisconsin Historical Collections*, August 28, 2006. Retrieved October 3, 2006. http://www.wisconsinhistory .org/odd/archives/002431.asp.

Wandschneider, John. "Report 2863 Hunter Observes Dark Figure." *Bigfoot Research Organization*. Retrieved August 4, 2010.

"Wisconsin Wild Pigs." *Wisconsin Outdoor*. Retrieved September 29, 2010. http://www.wisconsinoutdoor.com/pigs.htm.

ABOUT THE AUTHOR

Author, researcher, and artist Linda S. Godfrey hunts for the strange from her home in southeast Wisconsin. A former teacher and award-winning newspaper reporter and columnist, she has written and co-authored many books on strange creatures and other oddities, including *Haunted Wisconsin: Ghosts and Strange Phenomena of the Badger State*, two books in Barnes & Noble's Weird Series, three volumes in Chelsea House's Legends, Mysteries, and the Unexplained Series, and *The Beast of Bray Road* and its sequels *Hunting the American Werewolf* and *The Michigan Dogman*. She has appeared on many radio and TV shows, such as History Channel's *Monsterquest*, *Inside Edition*, Canada's *Northern Mysteries*, *Coast to Coast A.M.*, Jeff Rense Radio, and Wisconsin Public Radio. She lives with her husband, youngest son, and dog Grendel.

Other Titles in the
Monsters Series

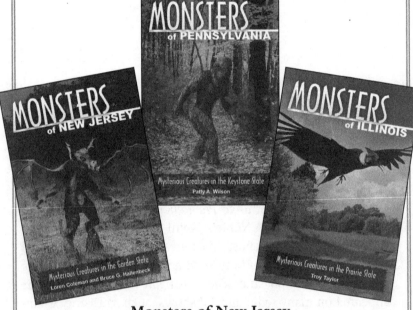

Monsters of New Jersey
by Loren Coleman & Bruce G. Hallenbeck
978-0-8117-3596-4

Monsters of Pennsylvania
by Patty A. Wilson
978-0-8117-3625-1

Monsters of Illinois
by Troy Taylor
978-0-8117-3640-4

WWW.STACKPOLEBOOKS.COM
1-800-732-3669